Presented by
Spencer P. Mead
to the
New York Public Library

LONGWOOD PUBLIC LIBRARY

Lenox Library, New York City
Compliments of the author

ADVANCE COPY.
GENEALOGICAL MATTER NOT INCLUDED.

PREFACE.

IN compiling the present volume, the author feels a deep sense of appreciation and gratitude to the late Rev. J. H. H. DeMille for the extensive researches made and the data collected by him concerning the Mead family, not only in this country, but also abroad, from which he has secured much valuable information, especially the genealogy, in the compilation of which the Rev. Mr. DeMille spent upwards of twenty years of his life, and this volume is published to perpetuate his memory among the different members of the family.

The author has also made reference to the History of *the Norman People*, published by King & Co., London, England; *History of Essex County, England*, by Thomas Wright, Esq., of Trinity College, Cambridge, England; *Old Colonial Records at Fairfield, Connecticut ; History of Dorchester, Massachusetts ; Huntington's History of Stamford, Connecticut ; Mead's History of Greenwich, Connecticut ;* Colonial Records of the New Haven Colony; *Trumbull's Colonial Records of Connecticut ; Hoadley's Colonial Records of Connecticut ; Hurd's History of Fairfield County, Connecticut ; Beer's History of Fairfield County, Connecticut; Military and Naval Service of Connecticut Men*, by Johnson; *Scharf's History of Westchester County, New York ; Bolton's History of Westchester County, New York ; Larned's History for Ready Reference ; History of Crawford County, Pennsylvania ;* Colonial and Revolutionary articles published in the *Greenwich Graphic*, Greenwich, Connecticut (1897–1898), and the *Tribune-Republican*, Meadville, Pennsylvania (in 1888); publications of the *New York Historical Society;* publications authorized by the General Assemblies of the States of Connecticut, New York, Vermont, and Pennsylvania; *New York in the Revolutionary War*, by the Board of Regents of the State of New York, and by the Hon. Jas. A. Roberts, Comptroller; *History of the Tenth Regiment Connecticut Volunteer Infantry*, by Brevet Brigadier-General John L. Otis; *Old Churches, Ministers, and Families of Virginia*, by Bishop Meade; *Hugh's American Ancestry*, and *Burke's Armory;* and has made extensive researches himself at the State Library at Hartford, Connecticut; Greenwich Library, Greenwich, Connecticut; the Astor and Lenox Libraries, and the Historical Society, New York City. He is especially indebted to the secretaries of the Society of Colonial Wars, and the Sons of the Revolution, for the many courtesies extended and valuable data furnished by them.

In collecting data for the present volume the author has in every instance selected the most reliable authorities and the best authenticated records and has endeavored to set forth a true statement of the facts as they existed in early days; but as there exists among the different branches of the family various traditions as to the progenitor of the family in this country and his immediate descendants, and as those traditions are at variance with historical facts, it is to be hoped that the family will not be too severe in their criticisms on learning that many of those traditions are mere fiction.

NEW YORK, November 12, 1901.

CONTENTS.

CHAPTER	PAGE
Preface	iii
I.—The Family in England	1
II.—The Family in New England	7
III.—The Family in Greenwich	14
IV.—The Family in New York State—Dutchess, Saratoga, Westchester, Chenango, Warren, and St. Lawrence Counties	26
V.—The Family in Vermont and St. Lawrence County, New York	32
VI.—The Family in Pennsylvania	35
VII.—The Family in Military and Civil Affairs during the Colonial Period	46
VIII.—The Revolutionary War	57
IX.—The War of 1812	87
X.—The War with Mexico, 1846-1848	94
XI.—The Civil War, 1861-1865	96
XII.—The Spanish-American War, 1898	114
XIII.—In Memoriam	116
Genealogy	123
Index to History	456
Index to Intermarriages	466

GENEALOGICAL MATTER NOT INCLUDED. ADVANCE COPY.

LIST OF ILLUSTRATIONS.

	PAGE
COAT OF ARMS . . . . . . *Frontispiece*	
OLD HOUSE AT INDIAN FIELD	14
OLD TAVERN, EBENEZER MEAD LANDLORD IN 1696 . .	18
THE FIRST BRICK HOUSE IN GREENWICH	52
THE HOUSE IN WHICH CAPTAIN SYLVANUS MEAD WAS SHOT BY COWBOYS	58
OLD HOMESTEAD OF BENJAMIN MEAD (2)	60
RESIDENCE OF THE LATE COLONEL THOMAS A. MEAD . .	69
GENERAL PUTNAM'S RIDE	71
TRACY HOUSE	73
PUT'S HILL IN 1895	84
MAJOR-GENERAL EBENEZER MEAD	91
RESIDENCE OF MILO MEAD	94
MAJOR DANIEL M. MEAD	99
CAPTAIN THOMAS R. MEAD	100
DR. DARIUS MEAD	116

ERRATA

Edward A., page 97, *should be* Edward N.
John B. T., Lieutenant, page 98, *should be* Adjutant.
General Plaister, page 105, *should be* Plaisted.
Colonel Shafter, page 107, *should be* Shaffer.
Insert March, third line, page 123.
Northfield, page 128, *should be* North Fairfield.
⁷Jared, page 267, *should be* ⁵Jared.
Grace Cornell, page 394, *should be* Cornwall.

HISTORY OF THE MEAD FAMILY.

CHAPTER I.

THE FAMILY IN ENGLAND.

THE very earliest traces of the Mead family are to be found in a history of *The Norman People, and their Existing Descendants in the British Dominions and the United States of America* published by King & Co., London, England, in 1874, in which its author has carefully traced the pedigrees of many of the English people, whose ancestry has heretofore been unauthenticated, and in many cases may have been founded on mere invention, but which now seems to be established beyond question. From that volume it appears that the name Mead is the English form of the Norman "de Prato," and to say that a family is Norman is nearly equivalent to saying that it is amongst the oldest of the old, and noblest of the noble.

In 1180-1195 there is to be found in the ancient Norman records the names of William, Robert, Matilda, Roger, and Reginald de Prato, and in 1198 the names of Richard and Robert de Prato. In 1199, Essex, England, occurs the name of Roger de Prato, and the same year also that of Walter de Prato in Hertford, England, and in 1272 those of Stephen and Peter de Prato, England.

Hervey de Prato, in 1200, in Normandy, was King John's

"faithful knight," and the custody of Rouen Castle was given to his brother.

The Norman "de Prato" was translated into the English, Mead, Meade, Mede, Meads.

The first of the Meade family who came originally from Somersetshire, into County Essex, in the reign of King Henry VI., and settled at Elmdon, according to the history of County Essex, was Thomas Meade, Esq. His son, Thomas Meade, Sergeant-at-Law in 1567, and constituted one of the Judges of the King's Bench, February 3, 1578, purchased Wendon Lofts, in whose family it continued for several generations, until it was sold by the coheiresses of John Meade, Esq., to Richard Chamberlain, Esq., of London, Sheriff of Sussex, in 1722. He also owned the Manors of Elmdonbury Hall, Dagworths, and Mounteneys, from whom it passed into the family of Bendish. Thomas Meade, of Elmdon, also had Reginald, who settled at Elmdon, and a second Thomas seated at Crishall, and two daughters.

Thomas Meade, of Wendon Lofts, married Joan Clamp, of Huntingdon, a widow, by whom he had Thomas, Robert, and Matthew, of whom the last two were never married. The father died in 1585, but this estate does not appear in the inquisition taken on that occasion. It, however, was in the possession of Sir Thomas Meade, the first son, at the time of his decease in 1617, who had holden it under Robert, Earl of Sussex. He had also large estates in Arkesden and Elmdon. He married Bridget, daughter of Sir John Brograve, Knight, of Hertfordshire, by whom he had Thomas, who died before him, John, Charles, George, Robert, and five daughters. He was succeeded, on his decease, by his eldest surviving son, Sir John Meade, Knight, who by Katharine, his lady, had Thomas, his successor, and two daughters. Thomas Meade, Esq., married Margaret, only daughter and heiress of Debney of Norfolk, by whom he had nine children. His successor was John, his eldest son, who, by his wife Jane, daughter of William Wardour, Esq., had John, who died an infant, Jane, who married John Whaley, merchant, of London, and Margaret, the wife of William Pytches, of Crishall.

In the chancel of the parish church at Elmdon, there is an ancient and magnificent monument erected to the memory of Thomas Meade, Esq., Justice of the King's Bench, by his most faithful wife, Joan, which informs us that he died in May, 1585.

In 1546, Edward Elrington and Humphrey, conveyed the Manor of Cristhall Grange to Edward Meade, Esq., and on his decease in 1577, he was succeeded by his son and heir, John Meade. The estate afterwards belonged to John Smith, Esq., of Upton.

The Manor of Great Easton was conveyed to John Meade, of Henham (family first mentioned in 1422), by William Fitch, and in his family it continued until the failure of heirs male, on the decease of John Meade of London, merchant, who died in 1689, and of his daughters Anne, in 1758, aged 87, and Elizabeth in 1761, aged 85. They had previously sold to Henry, the youngest brother of their father, the estate of Dutton Hill. Of the three sons of John Meade, of Henham, John, Robert, and George, the last had Nortofts, in Finchingfield, who kept his first court there in April, 1593. John succeeded his father on his decease in 1602, having married Ellen, daughter of Nicholas Colin, of Broxted, by whom he had Thomas of Henham, whose son John was of Matching, John, to whom he gave Dutton Hill, also Robert and William; he died in 1614. John of Dutton Hill, his second son, married Jane, daughter of John Glascock of Rowell, by whom he had his son and heir, John Mead, Gent. (final "e" omitted), who married Elizabeth, daughter and coheiress of Robert Samford of Chapel, by whom he had fourteen children of whom there survived him, on his death, John, Robert, Philip, William, Elizabeth, Anne, and Esther.

George Meade of Nortofts, married Dorothy, daughter of Sir Thomas Wendy, Knight, of Haslingfield, in Cambridgeshire, by whom he had John, and Elizabeth, wife of Sir Samuel Brown, one of the Justices of the Common Pleas. Besides the Manor of Nortofts, and one messuage, called Sculpius, a parcel of the said Manor, he had other estates in the parish, of which, by his will dated the 24th day of March, 1629, he devised to his wife Dorothy, a part during her life in recompense of her dower or jointure, and the remainder to his son and his wife. He died April 3, 1629, and was buried in the chancel of the church.

On the north wall of Marlborough church, County Leicester, on a monument of black marble, with the coat of arms, a chevron between three pelicans, appears the following inscription:

> "Near this place is interred the body of James Mead with his forefathers, Esquires.
> Also the body of Henry, son of James Mead. He married Ann, daughter of William Croft, of Peckleton, Esq.
> Also the body of William, son of Henry Mead, who married Elizabeth, daughter of Charnell Petty of Tetsworth, in Oxfordshire, Esquire.
> Also the body of Charnell, son of William Mead, who married Elizabeth, daughter of William Hewitt, of Stretton, Esquire.
> Also the body of William, son of Charnell Mead, who married Susannah, daughter of Matthew Floyer, of Heints, in Staffordshire, Esquire.
> Also the body of William, son of William Mead, who married Elizabeth, daughter of Edward Wilson, Rector of Milston, with an infant."

Many distinguished individuals have been in the Mead family of England, among them the Rev. Matthew Mead and his son, Dr. Richard Mead. The former was a celebrated non-conformist divine in the reign of Charles I. He was descended from a reputable family of Buckinghamshire, where he was born in 1629. Of his early life no account is preserved. He was a most sterling and eminent man, of strong concentrative powers of mind, and an independent thinker. He went in 1658 to Holland, returned in 1674, built a church in Stepney, and died there October 16, 1699.

His son, Dr. Richard Mead, was born at Stepney, August 11, 1673. He received his early education in Rome, under his father, and a private tutor, Mr. John Nesbit. In 1688 he was placed under the care of Mr. Thomas Singleton, and in the following year under the celebrated Grævius, at Utrecht. He took up the study of the classics and philosophy, and in 1692 removed to Leyden, where he remained three years, devoting himself to the study of medicine, and where he was cotemporary with Boerhave, then a student. In the year 1695, having completed the usual course of study at Leyden, he, in company with his brother Samuel and others, travelled in Italy, and while at Florence, had the good fortune to discover the *mensa isiaca* which for many years had been given up as lost. He took the degree of Doctor of Philosophy and Physics at Padua, August 16, 1695, and then visited Naples and Rome, and returned to England about midsummer, 1696. He settled at Stepney, in the house where he was born.

In 1702 Dr. Mead came before the public as an author, by the publication of his *Mechanical Account of Poisons*. This work was received with great interest, and at once established his reputation. He was elected Fellow of the Royal Society in 1704, one of the Council in 1706, and Vice-President in 1707. On May 5, 1703, he was elected Physician to St. Thomas's Hospital, and removed from Stepney to Crutched Friars, and afterwards to Austin Friars.

On December 7, 1707, the University of Oxford conferred on him the degree of Doctor of Medicine, and he thereafter presented himself for examination before the Censors' Board of the College of Physicians, underwent the usual examinations, and was admitted a Candidate, June 25, 1708, and a Fellow, April 9, 1710. He was Censor 1716, 1719, and 1724, and Harweian Orator in 1723.

After the accession of George II. Dr. Mead was appointed Physician in ordinary to the King, an office he continued to hold until his death, February 16, 1754. He was buried in the Temple Church, and a monument has been erected to his memory in Westminster Abbey.

Dr. Mead was married twice. By his first wife, Ruth Marshe, he had eight children. One of his daughters was married to Sir Edward Wilmot, Bart., an eminent physician. His second wife was Anne, daughter of Sir Rowland Alston, Bart.

COAT OF ARMS.

The coat of arms is thus described: Sa. a chev. betw. three pelicans or. vuln. gu.

Explanation:
- Sa., the color is sable, *i. e.*, black.
- Chev., a chevron represented as two rafters of a house joined together and descending in the form of a pair of compasses to the extremities of the shield.
- Or., signifies gold, and in engraving is represented by small dots.
- Three pelicans vuln. gu., *i. e.*, wounding themselves, according to the old tradition that the pelican picked its own breast to nourish its young.
- Crest, an eagle displayed.
- Motto: Semper Paratus—Always Ready.

CHAPTER II.

THE FAMILY IN NEW ENGLAND.

IN 1635 there arrived in Massachusetts many ships with passengers from England, and among those arrivals is found the name of Goodman Mead (called Gabriel Mead), who was born in 1587, and died March 12, 1666, aged 79 years. He was probably married twice, his second wife being Johanna, the daughter of James Bates. The latter was born in 1582, and died in 1655. He sailed from Lydd, County Kent, England, in the ship *Elizabeth* Captain Stagg, in April 1635, and it is supposed his son-in-law, Goodman Mead, was in the same vessel. Richard Bates (son) lived at Lydd, in County Kent, England, from whence the family is supposed to have come.

Gabriel (or Goodman) Mead left surviving him his widow, Johanna, and the following children: Israel, born in 1637, David, Lydia, Experience, Sarah, and Patience.

Recent researches seem to indicate that *William Mead*, the ancestor of the Fairfield County and the Greenwich, Connecticut, Meads, was a brother of Gabriel (or Goodman) Mead, and that they both came from England on the same ship, *Elizabeth*, April, 1635; furthermore, the coats of arms of the two are identical.

Goodman Mead remained in Massachusetts and is the ancestor of the Massachusetts Meads. *William*, however, followed the tide of emigration, which at that time was toward the

Connecticut Valley. The first English settlement of Connecticut was made at Windsor in October, 1633, and another settlement was made at Wethersfield soon after where *William* probably first settled, and in 1641, he removed to Stamford with several others from Wethersfield.

On the 18th day of July, 1640, Captain Daniel Patrick and Robert Feaks, as agents for the New Haven Colony, landed on Greenwich Point which the Indians called " Monakewego," and purchased from them that part of Petuquapaen lying between the Asamuck and the Patomuck Rivers, as described by the following deed:

Wee Amogerone, Sachem of Asamuck, and Rammatthone, Nawhorone, Sachems of Patomuck, have sould unto Robert Feaks and Daniell Patricke all theire rights and interests in all ye severall lands betwene Asamuck River and Patomuck, which Patomuck is a littel river which divideth ye bounds betwene Capt. Turner's Perchase and this, except ye neck by ye indians called Monakewego, by us Elizabeth Neck, which neck is ye peticaler perchace of Elizabeth Feaks, ye sd Robt Feaks his wife, to be hers and her heaires or assigns, forever, or else to be at ye disposal of ye aforementioned purchasers forever, to them and theire heaires, executors or assigns, and theye to enjoy all rivers, Islands, and ye severall naturall adjuncts of all ye forementioned places, neigther shall ye indians fish within a mille of aney english ware, nor invite nor permit aney other indians to sett down in ye forementioned lands; in consideration of which lands ye forementioned purchasers are to give unto ye above named sachems twentie five coates, whereof theye have reserved eleven in part payment; to witness all which, theye have hereunto sett theire hands this 18 July 1640.

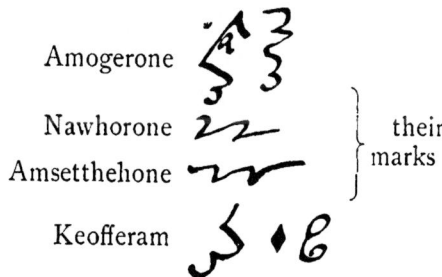

Witness:
  Robert A. Heusted,
                his
  Andrew   ⌒   Messenger,
            mark

Rasobibitt

Saponas

Whonehorn

Akeroque   (their marks)

Pauonohas

Powiatoh

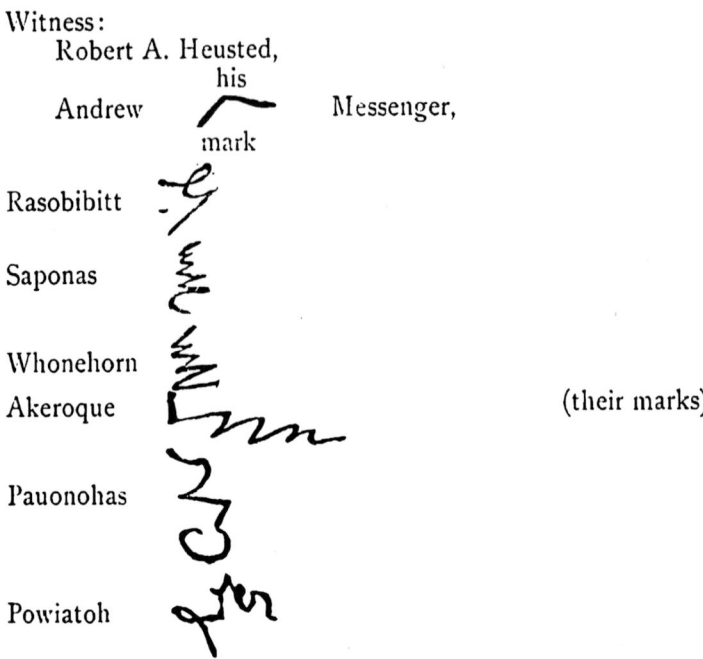

Keofferam hath sould all his right in ye above sd to Jeffere Ferris.
Witness:
  Richard Williams
  Angell Heusted.

They immediately located on a portion of the property and proceeded to form a settlement.

The Captain Turner referred to in the above deed is the party who, as agent for the New Haven Colony, first purchased from the Indians on the first day of July, 1640, lands now lying in the Town of Stamford. This tract was afterwards sold, November fourth of the same year, to Andrew Ward and Robert Coe, representatives of about twenty-two families of Wethersfield, but the first settlement of Stamford was not commenced by them until the spring of 1641, or nearly a year after Captain Patrick and Robert Feaks had settled at Old Greenwich (now Sound Beach), and among the first forty-two land proprietors of Stamford, Connecticut, we find the name of *William Mead*. The following is a copy of the entry in the *Stamford Town Records :*

> Dec. 7, 1641, William Mayd (Mead) received from the Town of Stamford, a homelot and five acres of land.

This *William* was the ancestor of the *Mead* family of Fairfield County, Connecticut, although family tradition declares that *John* was, also of eastern New York, western Vermont, and Meadville, Pennsylvania. There is record of three children, but there probably were four, including a son who died in 1658. They were as follows:

> JOSEPH, b. in 1630, married Dec. 4, 1654, Mary Brown of Stamford, d. May 3, 1690. He was the ancestor of the Ridgefield and North Fairfield County Meads, and had Zachariah, Joseph, Daniel, Elisha, Richard, and Mary.
>
> MARTHA, b. about 1632, who married John Richardson of Stamford. No further traces have been found.
>
> JOHN (1), b. about 1634, who married Hannah Potter of Stamford, probably in 1657, d. February 5, 1699. He was the ancestor of the Greenwich Meads, and had John (2), Joseph, Hannah, Ebenezer, Jonathan, David, Benjamin, Nathaniel, Samuel, Abigail, and Mary.

Tradition in the family also declares that Joseph died young, or if he lived, went South, and became the progenitor of the Virginia "Meade Family." Researches, however, prove the facts to be different. The Virginia Meades are in no wise connected with the Connecticut Meads, but are descended from Andrew Meade (anciently written Meagh), born in County Kerry, Ireland, in the latter part of the seventeenth century. He came to this country about 1728 and settled in Nansemond County, Virginia, where he died in 1745.[1] Colonel Richard Kidder Meade, Revolutionary soldier, served on General

---

[1] *Old Churches, Ministers, and Families of Virginia*, by Bishop Meade, of the Protestant Episcopal Church of Virginia.

The Family in New England.

Washington's staff; Rt. Rev. William Meade, D.D., late Bishop of the Protestant Episcopal Church of Virginia, and Richard Kidder Meade (2), of Petersburg, Virginia, Member of Congress, 1847 to 1853, are of this line.

The following record of some of the proceedings of the Court of Magistrates held at New Haven, shows that both *William* and his two sons, Joseph and John, settled here long before 1660, which is declared by family tradition to be the date of their settlement.

> 1654, October 18. Joseph Mead of Stamford, testifies on behalf of his sister Martha, the wife of John Richardson.
>
> 1656, May 26. John Mead, of Stamford, enters an action of ye case against Richard Law, of Stamford.
>
> 1656, May 26. Richard Law, of Stamford, complained of John Mead, of Stamford.
>
> 1656, May 26. Jno. Waterbury complained of John Mead.
>
> 1657, March 25. Joseph Mead, of Stamford, again a witness.
>
> 1657, March 27. A Petition from John Mead was presented desiring the Court to remitt the fine of ten pounds laide upon him last year.
>
> 1657, March 27. A Petition from *William Mead*, on behalf of John Richardson (his son-in-law), was presented, desiring the Court that the fine of ten pounds laide upon him be abated.

The two sons, Joseph and John, in the spring of 1657 removed to Hempstead, Long Island (several families from Stamford having formed the first settlement there in 1644), where the following records further show that Joseph did not die young.

> 1658. Joseph Mead, 3 milch cows, taxes 41 proportion.
>
> 1658. John Mead, 2 milch cows, taxes 19½ proportion.
>
> 1658. Joseph Mead, was Assistant Justice of Hempstead.
>
> 1659, February 3. The Town of Hempstead paid Joseph Mead nine shillings for a voyage from Stamford to

Fairfield to see about procuring a minister, with letters from Hempstead to the Rev. Mr. Wakeman.

From the last entry taken from the *Records of the Town of Hempstead*, it will be seen that Joseph returned to Stamford during the latter part of the year 1658, or the early part of 1659, otherwise his expenses would probably have been paid from Hempstead to Fairfield, instead of Stamford to Fairfield; moreover we find in the court records of the New Haven Colony :

1659, May 25. Joseph Mead, of Stamford, a witness.

1660, October 15. Joseph Mead, of Stamford, a witness, and from testimony given by him in Court, it appears that he was born in 1630.

1660, October 17. Joseph Mead, of Stamford, appeared as Attorney for Abraham Frost.

1662. Joseph Mead, Richard Hardey, who was the father-in-law of John Mead (2), and others, declared to be freemen of the Colony of Connecticut by the Assembly, and Mr. Gould was authorized "to guie them ye oath of freedom, at ye next Court in Fairfield."

Joseph, however, finally located permanently in Greenwich soon after his brother John bought land there in 1660. He was representative from Greenwich in the Colonial Assembly, 1669–1671. In the year 1672, we find among the list (*Greenwich Town Records*) of the first twenty-seven proprietors of Horseneck (Greenwich) the name of Joseph Mead. He died in Greenwich on the third day of May, 1690, sixty years of age, as appears from " Petition of ye widow and children of Joseph Mead, of Greenwich, who died without will May 3, 1690. Said petition is made by ye advise of our louving Unckle, John Mead, Sr." The petition was signed by Joseph Mead, Daniel Mead, Elisha Mead, and Mary Mead (her mark). He left children as follows: Zachariah, Joseph, Daniel, Elisha, Richard, and Mary.

Family tradition also declares that *John*, a son of Dr.

Richard Mead, settled in Greenwich in 1642, and was the progenitor of the Greenwich Meads, but reference to preceding pages of this volume shows how absurd this assertion is, and from which it will be seen that Dr. Richard Mead was not born until 1673, long after the traditional John is alleged to have settled in Greenwich, Connecticut.

CHAPTER III.

THE FAMILY IN GREENWICH.

OF *William*, the ancestor of all the Fairfield County Meads, very little concerning him, except that already mentioned, has been found. His wife died in Stamford, September 16, 1657. No record of his death has as yet been found.

John (1) removed from Hempstead, Long Island, to Old Greenwich (now Sound Beach) in 1660, and purchased land from Richerd Crab, October 26th, as will appear from the following deed as given on the town records:

These presents witnesseth an agreement made betwene Richerd Crab, of Grenwich, on ye one side, and John Mead, of Heamstead, on Long Island, on ye other side, viz.: Ye said Richerd Crab hath sould unto ye sd John Mead all his houses and Lands, yt sd Richerd Crab hath in Grenwich with all ye Apurtenances, Rights, & Privileges, & Conveniences, yt Doth belong unto ye sd houses & Lands, or shall here after belong unto them, viz.: ye house yt Richerd Crab liveth in, ye house yt Thomas Studwell liveth in, with ye Barne yt is on ye side of ye hye waye; also ye home lott yt ye house stands on, being bounded with a fence lying about them on ye northwest, against ye house lott; also Eightene Acres of Land in Elizabeth neck, more or less, being bounded by ye sea on ye east and southeast, and a fence on ye west, northwest, and ye north.

Also ye Rig, with 5 acres of Meadow lying in it, more or less; ye rig being bounded by ye Sea on ye southeast, william low on ye east, and ye fence on ye northwest, & north ye hye waye & hethcut's & angell Heusteds on ye west; also 3 acres of meadow in ye long meadow, & 1 acre of meadow by Ferris, bounded by Jeffere Ferris land on ye southeast, and ye cove

OLD HOUSE AT INDIAN FIELD, WHICH WAS OCCUPIED BY JONAS MEAD DURING THE REVOLUTIONARY WAR AND FREQUENTLY PILLAGED BY TORIES AND COWBOYS.

on ye west and northwest; also 5 acres of meadow in myanos neck. all ye above spesiffied I do hereby acknoledge to have sould unto ye above sd John Mead, his heaires and asignes, fully and freely to be possest forever, and for ye quiet and full performance hereof, I have hereunto subscribed my hand, anno 1660, October 26 Daye.

RICHERD CRAB.

Adam Mott,   } Witnesses.
Robt. Williams, }

John Mead (1) married Hannah, daughter of William Potter of Stamford. Her father afterwards owned Shippan Point, and through her he received a considerable amount of property.

The following anecdote, which has been preserved by tradition, shows his character: One day when he was quite an old man, as he was going for his grist on horseback to the mill at Dumpling Pond, before he reached the Mianus River he overtook an old Quaker jogging slowly along, loaded with a heavy budget. In a real spirit of kindness he offered to take the Quaker's load upon his horse, and thus give him a lift on his journey. "No," replied the Quaker, "thee don't get my bundle, for I can read men's thoughts. Thee wants to get my bundle, and then thee 'll run off. Thee don't get my bundle." "Very well," was the simple reply, and so they went slowly on together. At last they came to the brink of the Mianus River. Here the Quaker was really in trouble. How to cross a river, two or three feet deep, dry shod, was quite a puzzle. But he gladly accepted a second offer of assistance from the horseman. The bundle was mounted in front, John in the middle, and the Quaker behind. Arriving at the centre of the river, in pretending to adjust his stirrup John caught the Quaker by the heel and gave him a gratuitous bath. Such treatment was too much, even for Quaker forbearance, and the victim, with his hands full of pebbles, would have taken summary vengeance, had not the other party threatened to put the bundle under a similar course of treatment. This threat, and the lecture following it, gradually cooled off the Quaker's anger. John informed him that all had been done for his good, to teach him a lesson. And the lecturer said he hoped the stranger would never again profess to read men's thoughts. "For," said he, "I asked you to ride, kindly in the first place, when you refused; but at the second time of asking, I really intended to do as I have just done." So saying, and tossing the bundle back, he rode on, leaving his companion to apply the moral as he thought best.

In 1670 John Mead (1) was propounded for a freeman of Greenwich by the Assembly, and was a member of the Assembly in 1679, 1680, and 1686.

The first settlement of the Town of Greenwich, as has been previously stated, was made at Elizabeth Neck (now Sound Beach), but about the year 1672 a number of persons, mostly living in the town, though some were from other colonies than Connecticut, purchased from the few Indians then living about the western part of the town, Miosehasseky (Horseneck), now Greenwich Borough. These purchasers were twenty-seven, and were styled the "27 proprietors of 1672." On the list as it appears in the *Greenwich Town Records* are found among the twenty-seven the names of

Joseph Mead, and John Mead (1).

In 1681 took place the earliest marriage that is recorded, although others must have preceded it, by the Rev. Jeremiah Peck, John Mead (2) to Miss Ruth Hardey, daughter of Richard Hardey.

In 1687 John Mead (2) was elected constable, then the most remunerative as well as the most important office in the gift of the townsmen.

On the list of legal voters at Horseneck for the year 1688, are found the following names:

Joseph Mead   John Mead (1)
Ebenezer Mead   John Mead (2)
Jonathan Mead   Joseph Mead, John Mead's son
    Joseph Mead, Joseph Mead's son.

A little previous to this time, however, about 1686, the Indians sold almost their last acre of land in the town to Ebenezer Mead (1). These lands were at the mouth of the Mianus River, on its western bank, and the original deed is now in the possession of the Hon. Whitman S. Mead, who resides on a part of the property, it having remained in the family ever since its purchase from the Indians. In 1691 it was voted to have a new meeting-house, and John Mead (1), John Mead (2), and others, were appointed a committee to procure materials and build the house. It was finally built upon a small rise of ground, northwest of the old burying-ground at Old Greenwich (Sound Beach), near where the present First Congregational Church now stands.

In 1693, May 12, occurred the death of John Mead (2), the acting constable, which was deeply lamented by the people. They called an extra town meeting, and passed resolutions deploring the loss of so estimable an officer and citizen. He was the grandson of the first settler, only about thirty-five years of age, and left surviving him, his widow and four children, as follows: John (3), Jonathan, Nathan, and Elizabeth. John (3) remained in Horseneck; Jonathan died in 1712, without issue, and Nathan settled at Amenia, Dutchess County, New York.

The tax list for the Town of Greenwich for the years 1694 and 1695 contains the following names, besides many others:

	l.	s.	d.
Benjamin Mead	87	0	0
Ruth Mead, widow of John Mead (2).	22	10	0
Daniel Mead	42	0	0
Zachariah Mead	30	0	0
Ebenezer Mead	103	10	0
Joseph Mead, the tanner	45	10	0

Jonathan Mead	45	0	0
Nathaniel Mead	30	0	0
Elisha Mead	38	0	0
Samuel Mead	87	10	0
Joseph Mead, not the tanner	25	0	0

In 1696 Ebenezer Mead was appointed by the town to keep "a place of publik entertainment for man and beast." The old tavern stood on the same site for nearly two hundred years, and has a history linked with Colonial and Revolutionary Wars. Many a thrilling episode occurred around its doors and within its quaint rooms. One night during colonial days, when some of the frivolous young people of the colony were holding a dance in the house, a besieging party of Puritans broke open the front door and drove them out like cattle, and the merry-makers retired in confusion. Jumping out of windows helter-skelter, they scattered in every direction before the clubs and invectives of the sad faced Puritans. It was here also during the early days of the French and Indian War that a company of young men were surprised by a press-gang, and several of them forced into the service.

The old tavern was built as were dwellings of those days. The laths were split with an axe from oak, and the nails were made by the village blacksmith. There was an immense wine closet in the cellar, where the choicest wines and liquors were kept that gladdened the hearts of ye travellers as well as ye soldiers.

General Putnam quaffed many a glass of Medford rum 't is said here, and frequently held conferences within its rooms with his fellow officers of the Revolution. It was a common thing for the soldiers, tories, and cowboys, to ride up to the east window—there was no fence about the lot—and gracefully stoop while on their horses and catch the welcome cup hastily handed by ye genial landlord, who gave them ye latest news of ye doings of ye British hereabouts, in answer to their hurried questions.

OLD TAVERN. EBENEZER MEAD LANDLORD IN 1696.

When Governor Tryon made his raid, February 26, 1779, he made his quarters at this old tavern, then kept by Henry Mead, and while he was waiting for his dinner a patriot crept slyly into an adjoining orchard and fired a ball through the clapboards, which whistled close by Governor Tryon's head and struck the mantel-piece, from which it rebounded upon the floor. This startled Tryon so much that he, without waiting for his dinner, gave immediate orders for a retreat.

An old Hessian sabre was found in the house about fifty years ago, and when it was torn down in July, 1886, to make room for the present Presbyterian Church, a number of relics were found. A board was disclosed near the big chimney, on which the name of Reuben Mead and the figures 1741 were printed in charcoal, and under the fireplace was uncovered another board, on which was a score, drawn with charcoal, of apples, potatoes, and whiskey. No doubt it was the account of ye jolly landlord with some of his neighbors. An English penny, dated 1701, a piece of blue cloth with brass buttons, a pair of Indian moccasins, a long old-fashioned fire shovel, a big brass strainer, and some other things were also found. Relic hunters watched the old tavern as it fell, piece by piece, and took away shingles and nails.

In 1699, February 5, occurred the death of John Mead (1) probably in his sixty-sixth year. He had been a prominent citizen, respected by all not only for his even temperament, but also for his energy and decision of character. The following are his children:

John (2), Joseph, Hannah, Ebenezer, Jonathan, David, Benjamin, Nathaniel, Samuel, Abigail, and Mary. He left two wills, both dated the sixteenth day of March, 1696. One devising his real property to his sons is recorded in the office of the Town Clerk of Greenwich, Connecticut, and the other making bequests of personal property to all his children is recorded in the *Fairfield Probate Records*. Both of these are curiosities of antiquity and are well worthy of being preserved. The following is a copy of his will relating to real property recorded at Greenwich, Connecticut:

KNOW ALL MEN BY THESE PRESENTS, yt I JOHN MEAD, SENIR, of grenwich in ye Collonie of Conecticut for ye Love goodwill & afection which I haue & beare towards my naturall Sonn John Mead of ye Towne of grenwich & Collonie aforesd, have giuen & granted & do by these presents fully Clearely and absolutely giue & grant unto my sd Sonn John Mead now deseased for his Sonn John Mead my grandsonn a sertaine Persale of Land and meadow Lying & being in grenwich bounded by ye Land yt I John Mead Senir. bought of John Bowers north & a line drawn from ye north east corner of ye Land I bought of Angell Heusted Jur. to a grate rock Lying in ye frunt fence, all ye Lands lying within this Compas with ye house as it is bounded:

Ye frunt of sd Land being Bounded upon thee hyewaye west, the Reare upon ye sea South East. Upon these considerations following I giue & grant fully Clearely & absolutely ye above mentioned lands to him, his heaires & asignes: Imprimis, yt hee fully Confirme yt contract yt was betwene his father & his Unckle Ebinezer Mead; 2lly yt hee pay to his Brothers Jonathan & Nathan Mead when they com to bee of cage five pounds to Each of them & to his Sister Elizabeth Mead fortie Shilings; Item, I giue & fully grant unto ye aforesd John two acres in ye home lott insted of yt which ye sd John his father, now deseased, had of me in ye Southfeild disposing of yt in ye Southfeild, as I see Convenient.

FURTHER KNOW ALL MEN BY THESE PRESENTS, yt I John Mead Senir. aforesd for ye Love goodwill & afection which I haue & beare towards my Naturall Sonn Joseph Mead of ye Towne of grenwich haue giuen & granted & by these presents do fully Clearely & absolutely giue & grant unto my sd Sonn Joseph Mead his heaires & asignes a sertaine Persale of Land & meadow, Lying in Myanos neck estemed seven acres be it more or Les, as it is Bounded; Item, I giue unto my sd Sonn Joseph Mead, his heaires & asignes, three acres of Land in Stanfford Southfeild neare ye uper gate be it more or Les, as it is Bounded.

FURTHER KNOW ALL MEN BY THESE PRESENTS, yt I John Mead Senir. aforesd for ye Love goodwill & afection which I haue and beare towards my Naturall Sonn Ebinezer Mead of ye Towne of grenwich aforesd haue giuen & granted & by these presents do fully, Clearely & absolutely giue & grant unto my sd Sonn Ebinezer his heaires & asignes a Persale of meadow in ye Hosack meadow, estemed two acres & an halfe be it more or Les, ye Bounds being known to ye sd Ebinezer.

FURTHER KNOW ALL MEN BY THESE PRESENTS, yt I John Mead Senir, aforesd for ye Love goodwill & afection which I haue & beare towards my Naturall Sonn Jonathan Mead of ye Towne of grenwich aforesd haue giuen & granted & by these presents do fully Clearely and absolutely giue & grant unto my sd Sonn Jonathan his heaires & asignes an home lott Layd out to mee at horseneck and all my Lands lying within horse neck feild & a Persale of Land Containing three acres more or Les, Lying at ye South East End of ye Widow Hows Lott.

FURTHER KNOW ALL MEN BY THESE PRESENTS, yt I John Mead Senir. aforesd for ye Love goodwill & afection which I haue & beare towards my Naturall Sonn Dauid Mead of ye Towne of Bedfford now in ye government of New Yorke, haue giuen & granted & by these presents do fully Clearely & absolutely giue & grant unto my sd Sonn Dauid Mead his heaires & asignes my whole acomidation Lying & being at Bedfford both Lands & meadows as it was granted to me.

FURTHER KNOW ALL MEN BY THESE PRESENTS, yt I John Mead Senir. aforesd for ye Love goodwill & afection which I haue & beare towards my Naturall Sonn Benjamen Mead of ye Towne of grenwich aforesd, haue giuen & granted & by these presents do fully Clearely and absolutely giue & grant unto my sd Sonn Benjamen those Persales of Land & meadows hereafter exprest, viz.: five acres of Land at Stickling brock as it is Layd out to mee, and all my Lands & meadow Lying & being at that place Commonly Cauled Coscob, as it is Layd out to mee & ten acres of upland above ye Road aded now to ye five.

FURTHER KNOW ALL MEN BY THESE PRESENTS, yt I John Mead Senir. aforesd for ye Love goodwill & afection which I haue & beare towards my Naturall Sonn Nathaniell Mead of ye Towne of grenwich aforesd haue giuen & granted & by these presents do fully Clearely & absolutely giue & grant unto my sd Sonn Nathaniell, his heaires & asignes an acre & Twentie rods of meadow in ye Southfeild, as it is Bounded: Likewise seven acres of Land Lying at a place cauled Croch; also two Thirds of ny Lands, as it shall bee Layd out of that Estate in Patrigs List.

FURTHER KNOW ALL MEN BY THESE PRESENTS, yt I John Mead Senir. aforesd for ye Love goodwill & afection which I haue & beare towards my Naturall Sonn Samll Mead of ye Towne of grenwich haue giuen & granted & by these presents do fully Clearely & absolutely giue & grant unto ye sd Samll Mead, his heaires & asignes all my Houseing with ye Orched: Item, all my Lands on ye East Side of ye Hyewaye by my House both meadow & Land & Plowing Land, Bounded by ye grate Rock yt lyeth in ye fence of ye Land of my Grand Sonn John Mead & upon a Streight line to ye North East Corner of ye meadow Land I John Mead aforesd Bought of Angell Heusted Jur.: Item, all my Land upon Elizabeth neck, as it is bounded: Item, all my alotment in ye Long meadow & all my meadow Lying by James Ferris, as it is Bounded, & ye peace of Land I Bought of Clement Buxton Lying in Stanfford Southfeild as it is Bounded & my alotment in Stanfford Eastfeild in Shipan, which was my father Potters, as it is Bounded; also yt Persale of Land I had of ye ouerseers of my father Potters Estate Lying within Stanfford bounds, frunting by ye Hye waye, by ye South feild, as it is Bounded.

FURTHER KNOW yt ye aforesd housing, Land & meadows I do frely giue to him sd Samll my Sonn, his heaires & asignes as aforesd, also a Persale of Land Lying by Gershom Lockwood, Bounded by ye Hye waye, next west upon ye Land of my Grand Sonn John Mead South East, which Persale of Land was not mentioned before. Provided yt ye sd Samll his heaires and asignes do well & honarably maintaine his mother with a Convenient roome in ye house such a roome as shee shall cheuse, & with such other Things as may be Sutable for her Comfortable Subsistence during her widdowhood & that hee pay out to his brother Nathaniell aforesd Twentie pounds in Provesion paye as it paseth from man to man amoungst us. Beginning ye Payment of it after my Desease & Paying five Pounds pr annum till tis Payde.

IN WITNESS WHEREOF, I haue hereunto sett my hand & Seale this 16 of March 1695-6.

his
JOHN + MEAD
mark.

SIGNED & SEALED IN PRESENCE OF US:
    SALLOMON TREAT,
    ZACKARIAH MEAD.

These aboue Writen Deads & seuerall Grants of Lands on both sides of this Paper was acnowlidged by ye granter John Mead Senir to bee his act & deed this 24 of March, 1697, in Stanfford before mee.   JONATHAN BELL,
Commissioner.

The Family in Greenwich.

On first thought it seems odd that two wills, the one devising real property, and the other bequeathing personal property, both executed the same day, should be valid; but this is explained by the fact that at that time wills devising real property had to be recorded in the town where the land was located, while those bequeathing personal property were only recorded in the Probate Court having jurisdiction, which in those early days was Fairfield.

The will making bequests of personal property to all his children, both sons and daughters, is therefore recorded in the *Fairfield Probate Records*. It is a very curious document, and is as follows:

WHEREAS, I, JOHN MEAD SENIR of grenwich in ye Collonie conecticut though at present in reasonable helth, yet being sencable of my bodyly weakness and Infirmities of ould eage and not Knowing the daye of my departure out of this world do make this my Last will & Testament in manner and form following:

First: I Comit my Soul into ye hands of Allmity God hopeing for Saluation from the Riches of His Grace through the allone merrits of Jesus. Also I Comit my body to ye Earth decently to be buried and there to rest unto the Resurection of the Just. And for my wuldly Est. boath Reall and personall, I dispose of it as followeth:

Imprimis: All my just debts and funerall Charges being paid by my wife whom I make my Sole Executrix of my will and I do will and bequeath unto my Eldest Sonn John Mead the Just Sum of five Shilings, besides what I haue alredy Giuen him to be paid by my Executrix.

2lly: My will is and I do will and bequeath unto my Sonn Joseph Mead ye Just sum of five Shilings besides what I haue alredy giuen him to be paid by my Executrix.

3lly: My will is and I do will and bequeath unto my Sonn Ebinezer Mead ye Just sum of five Shilings besides what I haue alredy giuen him to be paid by my executrix.

4lly: My will is and I do will and bequeath unto my Sonn Jonathan Mead ye Just sum of five Shilings besides what I haue alredy giuen him to be paid by my Executrix.

5lly: My will is and I do will and bequeath unto my Sonn

Dauid Mead ye Just sum of five Shilings besides what I haue alredy giuen him to be paid by my Executrix.

6lly: My will is and I do will and bequeath unto my Sonn Benjamen Mead ye Just sum of five Shilings besides what I haue alredy giuen him to be paid by my Executrix.

7lly: My will is and I do will and bequeath unto my Sonn Nathaniell Mead ye Just sum of five Shilings besides what I haue alredy giuen him to be paid by my Executrix.

8lly: My will is and I do will and bequeath unto my Sonn Sam'll Mead ye Just sum of five Shilings besides what I haue alredy giuen him to be paid by my Executrix.

9lly: My will is and I do will and bequeath unto my daughter Hannah Scoful ye full & Just sum of five Shilings to be paid by my Executrix.

10lly: My will is and I do will and bequeath unto my daughter Abagaile ye Just sum of five Shilings to be paid by my Executrix.

11lly: My will is and I do will and bequeath unto my daughter Mary ye Just sum of five Shilings to be paid by my Executrix.

12lly: My will is and I do will and bequeath unto my dear and loueing Hannah Mead all my Estate Reall and Personall which I haue not disposed of to my Children Either by Will or gifts. She paying the seuerall Legacies as before Exprest for her Comfortable Subsistanc in this world and to be wholly at her disposal to distribute.

Lastly: My will is that my Sonns Joseph, Ebinezer, and Benjamen be ouerseers to se yt this my Last Will & Testament be fully & Carefully performed to see yt their mother be Carefully prouided for.

IN CONFERMATION yt this is my Last will & Testament, I haue hereunto Sett my hand and Seale this 16 of March, 1695-6.

his
JOHN + MEAD
mark

SIGNED & SEALED IN PRESENCE OF US:
SALLOMON TREAT
ZACKARIAH MEAD.

The aboue written Will was acnolidged by John Mead Senir. to bee his own free act & deed this 24th March, 1697 in Stanfford before me.

JONATHAN BELL.
Commissioner.

John Mead (1), it is supposed, was buried in an old burying-ground a little southwest from the old one yet in existence on Greenwich Point. All traces of this burial place are now removed, the tombstones having been taken to build fences, and the ground often ploughed over without any respect for those who lie sleeping there.

Up to 1703 all town meetings had been held in Greenwich "Old Town," but in that year it was voted that they should be held one half of the time at Horseneck. Also about this time there was quite an emigration from the old settlement to the western and northwestern parts of the town, so that in 1704 the settlement had become so large that it was found impossible for one minister to attend to the wants of the inhabitants at both Horseneck and Old Greenwich; therefore, in 1705 an agreement "betwene ye Inhabitants on ye East sid of Myanos River and ye Inhabitants of sd Grenwich on ye West sid of sd Myanos River" was entered into, whereby the town was divided into two societies. The First Society being on "ye East sid of sd Myanos River," and the Second being on "ye West sid of sd Myanos River."

At a town meeting held in Greenwich at Horseneck, June 15, 1716, "Mr. Ebinezer Mead and others were chozen to lay out the landing and highway on the Northside of horseneck brook."

CHAPTER IV.

THE FAMILY IN NEW YORK STATE—DUTCHESS, SARATOGA, WESTCHESTER, CHENANGO, WARREN, AND ST. LAWRENCE COUNTIES.

NATHAN MEAD, the third son of John (2), removed to Dutchess County, New York, and settled at Amenia. He died February 14, 1777, leaving two children, Nathan and Job (1); the latter was born in 1735, and married Mercy King. Job (1) located at Nine Partners, and contributed toward the building of the " Red Meeting-House," which was built in 1758; he served as captain in the Revolutionary War, and died April 23, 1819. His family was as follows: Rebecca, Job (2), who served in the War of 1812, Nathan, Mercy, and Joshua.

Jonathan Mead (2), born in Horseneck, the eldest son of Jonathan (1), who was the fourth son of John (1), removed to Dutchess County, New York, and settled at Nine Partners. His children settled in Chenango County, New York, and in Wyoming, Northumberland, and Crawford Counties, Pennsylvania.

[5] Zachariah, born about 1735, of the Joseph line, son of [4] Nehemiah, who was the sixth son of the second [3] Joseph, settled at Ballston, Saratoga County, New York, before the Revolutionary War, and probably had [6] Israel and [6] Isaiah; [6] Isaiah had [7] Ebenezer who had [8] Hosea.

In the early part of 1752 the First Presbyterian Society of

South Salem decided to call a minister; accordingly a convention was held at Salem on the nineteenth day of May, 1752, and the Rev. Solomon Mead of Greenwich was ordained.

The upper part of Westchester County was almost a wilderness when "Parson Solomon," as he was frequently called, undertook the task of planting an independent church at that place and for some time he was in the habit of riding up weekly from Greenwich on horseback. His first residence stood on the property of Mr. William Hoyt, near the home of his grandson, the late Richard Mead; but a few years before his death he removed to the residence of his son, Martin.

The Rev. Solomon Mead was the fifth son of Ebenezer Mead (2) born in Horseneck, December 25, 1725, graduate of Yale College, class of 1748. He married January 1, 1755, for his first wife Hannah, daughter of the Rev. Dr. Benjamin Strong, minister at Stanwich, Connecticut, and had by her two children, Theodosia and Andrew. His first wife died October 20, 1761. He married second, Hannah, daughter of Thomas C. Clark of Waterbury, Connecticut. This marriage took place in the depth of winter. He rode the fifty miles from South Salem on horseback, but arrived so late that all the guests had departed. Some, however, were recalled and the pair were married at midnight. After the ceremony their wedding tour consisted of a horseback ride, she on a pillion behind, as was the custom in those days, from Waterbury to South Salem, in a terrible snowstorm, in order not to disappoint those who had been invited to a reception at South Salem. His children by his second wife were: Clark, of Lewisboro, and Martin, of Lewisboro. He died on the fifth day of September, 1812, in the eighty-seventh year of his age, having been pastor of the South Salem Presbyterian Church for over forty-eight years, having resigned in 1800 on account of ill-health caused by paralysis.

His tombstone is to be seen in the burying-ground in South Salem, where many others of the Mead family lie buried. The inscription on the stone is as follows :

> "Memory of the
> Rev. Solomon Mead
> First Pastor of the Presbyterian
> Church in this place, Æ 86.
> He had the charge of this people
> 48 years,
> Ob. September, 1812.
> While marble monuments decay,
> The Righteous live in endless day,
> And earthly temples turn to dust,
> Blest is the memory of the just."

Enoch Mead, second son of Ebenezer Mead (3) and brother of Major Ebenezer Mead (4) of the War of 1812, was born in Horseneck, April 9, 1756, and married in his twentieth year, February 1, 1776, Jemima, daughter of Caleb Mead, also in her twentieth year, born August 12, 1756. He and his bride, as a wedding tour, took a trip through Massachusetts on horseback, and on their return settled about half a mile south of Lake Waccabuc on the New York and Albany post road. Here he built a log house in which was born his eldest son, Solomon, but from this he soon moved to the house still standing (built during the Revolutionary War), which is now owned and occupied by his descendants, and known as "Elmdon."

Enoch Mead at one time during the Revolutionary War was colonel's clerk in Lieutenant-Colonel John Mead's Regiment. His family consisted of nine children. He died September 10, 1807, and his widow April 4, 1837.

Scharf in his *History of Westchester County, N. Y.*, states that "Colonel Enoch Mead at one time during the Revolutionary War served on the staff of his brother, General Ebenezer Mead." This is a gross misrepresentation, as official records show that if this Ebenezer Mead served in the Revolutionary War at all, he served as a private only. After the war, however, he gained distinction as a training master in the militia, and rose to the rank of Major-General, but served as Major in the War of 1812.

⁶ Elias S. Mead, born March 21, 1801, of the Joseph line as follows : ¹ William, ² Joseph (1), ³ Joseph (2), ⁴ Israel, ⁵ John. Elias at the time of his mother's death was but eleven years old, when a neighbor evinced great partiality for him, and desired his father to give or bind the boy to him, promising to make him his heir, as he had no children of his own. His father did so, believing it to be for the best interest of the child, as the man was reputed wealthy. Unfortunately, however, the man soon formed intemperate habits, and moved from place to place, wasting his wealth rapidly. In his travels he stopped a short time at South Bainbridge, Chenango County, New York, where he formed some very pleasant acquaintances and sincere friends, so that when his guardian began to prepare for another move, he resolved to leave the man who had failed to fulfil his part of the contract by neglecting entirely to send him to school. The advice of his friends strengthened this resolution, and when his adopted parents took their leave of South Bainbridge, he remained. He gained in time many warm friends, and by industry and application obtained what was then considered a good common school education.

When twenty-two years of age he married Sophia F. Williams, who was in her eighteenth year. She died July 18, 1842, leaving a family of six children. Three years later he married Beulah Applington, and had by her two children. One died at three years of age, and the other, Ella J., acquired considerable reputation as an elocutionist and dramatic reader. He died in South Bainbridge, November 13, 1859.

Jonathan Mead (3), born in Horseneck about 1727, the eldest son of Jonathan (2), who was the eldest son of Jonathan (1), the fourth son of John (1), was married in 1758 to Sarah Guernsey, born in 1736. He went with his father to Nine Partners, Dutchess County, New York, and afterwards removed to Chenango County, New York. He died February 10, 1804, leaving him surviving the following children: Amos, Jonathan (4), Ruth, Sarah, Samuel, Thompson (Colonel), who served in the War of 1812, and Rachel.

James Mead, born in Horseneck, January 8, 1769, the fifth son of Jeremiah, who was the third son of Caleb, who was the eldest son of Ebenezer, the third son of John (1), removed to the Town of Chester, Warren County, New York, about the year 1795. He married, the following year, Anna Potter, of the same county, born June 26, 1777, and settled in the northern part of the Town of Chester upon wild land, where he remained until his death, which occurred September 16, 1837. His wife survived him thirty-three years and attained the ripe age of ninety-three. They left a large family consisting of ten children, eight of whom were still living in 1873; the oldest was seventy-six, the youngest fifty-three, and their combined ages were five hundred and thirty-nine years. Three years previous, while the mother and brother James were living, their united ages were six hundred and sixty-six years.

Jasper Mead, born in Horseneck, June 16, 1760, the eldest son of Nathaniel, who was the second son of John (3), who was the eldest son of John (2), the eldest son of John (1), removed to the Town of Chester, Warren County, New York, about the year 1799. He married Sarah, daughter of Titus Mead, born March 27, 1762, by whom he had Rachel, Bush, Titus, Sally, Shadrach, Andrew, Nathaniel, and Charity.

The St. Lawrence County family is descended from the Vermont branch. (See Vermont family.)

There are a great many Meads living in and around Lake Waccabuc, Westchester County, New York, and elsewhere in the eastern part of the State, who claim that they are descended from the Horseneck (Greenwich) family, but for the lack of complete family records are unable to trace their genealogy back to that place. The author after years of research has also been unable to find the connecting link, or identify them with any branch of this family, but believes they are undoubtedly descended from Daniel and Richard, who were children of the first Joseph.

CHAPTER V.

THE FAMILY IN VERMONT AND ST. LAWRENCE COUNTY, NEW YORK.

TIMOTHY MEAD (1), the fourth son of Jonathan (1), who was the fourth son of John (1), was born in Horseneck, but moved from there with his family before 1754 to a place called Nine Partners, from the first settlers who were nine in number, in Dutchess County, New York, and located a few miles from his cousin, Nathan.

During the year 1769, Timothy (1) with five sons, Timothy (2), Zebulon, James (Colonel), Stephen, Ezra, and one daughter, emigrated from Nine Partners to Rutland County, Vermont. Three of the sons, Zebulon, James (Colonel), and Ezra, settled on Otter Creek, West Rutland, between what is now known as Mead's Mills, or Centre Rutland, and Sutherland Falls. These were the first white people that ever settled in Vermont. Colonel James on the thirtieth of September, 1769, made his first purchase of land in Rutland. There were seventy rights in the whole town, one right containing three hundred and fifty acres. He bought twenty rights for £100 and sold ten the same day for £40, retaining ten rights, or thirty-five hundred acres. The first night Colonel James spent in Rutland, he, with his wife, occupied an Indian wigwam on the banks of Otter Creek, a short distance below Centre Rutland, the Indians kindly vacating it and giving them possession. That same fall he built a log house half a mile west of Centre Rutland near the banks of West Creek. The following year, 1770, he was forty years old, with a wife and ten children. The first white child born in Rutland, Vermont, is said to have been William, born September 24, 1770, the eleventh child of Colonel James. The twelfth and youngest child James, was born December 12, 1773. William, the eleventh child, moved from Vermont to Ohio. He often used to say that he remembered riding behind his mother, on horseback, to a place of safety at the time of the battle of Bennington, August 16, 1777, and that his brother James was carried by his mother in front, while he held on behind. He died at Granville, Ohio, November 24, 1854, and on his tombstone is the following inscription:

"Capt.
William Mead
died
Nov. 24, 1854,
aged 84 years.
He was the first white child born
in Rutland."

His family consisted of three children.

Mrs. Mead died May 11, 1823, aged ninety-two. The following is on her tombstone in the old cemetery at West Rutland:

"Mercy Mead relict of Col. James Mead."

Stephen, the fourth child of Timothy (1), settled on Otter Creek three miles below Sutherland Falls, in the Town of Pittsford. He had a family of thirteen children.

The daughter of Timothy (1) married one of the Stark family.

Zebulon and Ezra, who also settled on Otter Creek, had families consisting of eleven and fourteen children respectively. Cary, the third son of Zebulon, married Judith Sampson. They moved to Ohio in 1808, and first settled in a cabin about five miles west of Granville, Licking County, near where the town of Alexandria now stands. They afterwards moved on to a farm about half a mile south of Granville. The next removal of this family was to what was then known as Cook's settlement, now the village of Appleton, where the parents died.

Timothy (2) settled in Manchester, Bennington County, Vermont and had a family of thirteen children. Henry Mead, the son of Jacob, who was the son of Timothy (2), was born in Manchester, Vermont, December 25, 1784, where he lived until 1805, when he went to Canton, St. Lawrence County, New York, which was nearly all wilderness at that time, there being only six families in that town. He began clearing a piece of land, but the mosquitoes and black flies were so thick that it was almost impossible to work. The only way he could work was to keep a bush in his hand, and each time he struck a blow with the axe, the leaves would brush the insects from his face. He stayed in Canton until 1806, when he returned to Vermont, remaining there until 1812. He served three months in the War of 1812 when he received his discharge and went back to Canton through fifty miles of woods on foot. He married in 1816, and settled on a farm in the southern part of the Town of Canton, where he spent the remainder of his life. His family consisted of ten children.

CHAPTER VI.

THE FAMILY IN PENNSYLVANIA.

AMONG others of note descended from the Greenwich family, there is the Hon. David Mead, the pioneer to the waters of French Creek, and one of the first settlers of the pleasant village which bears his name, Meadville, Pennsylvania. He was born at Hudson, New York, January 17, 1752. His father, Darius, the son of Jonathan (2), who was the eldest son of Jonathan (1), the fourth son of John (1), was a native of Connecticut, as was also his mother, whose maiden name was Ruth Curtis, who had, besides David, Asahel, John, Ruth, Darius, Betsy, and Joseph. Darius Mead purchased a farm in Hudson to which he removed before the birth of any of his children, and there resided until his eldest son, this David, had arrived at his twenty-first year. He then sold his estate and left New York for Pennsylvania, and in connection with his son became proprietor, under a Pennsylvania title, to some valuable lands in Wyoming County; but in consequence of adverse claims under Connecticut titles, they with the rest of the family took up their residence on the western bank of the North Branch of the Susquehanna River, about six miles above the Town of Northumberland, a few years before the commencement of the Indian depredations in that region in 1778.

About the year 1774, David Mead married Agnes, daughter of John and Janet Wilson of Northumberland County, by whom he had nine children.

At an early period in the Revolutionary struggle, the incursions of the Indians were becoming so frequent and bloodthirsty on the frontiers of Pennsylvania, as to put the inhabitants to flight. For a long time during the war, numerous were the scenes of savage bloodshed and cruelty, and great was the distress of the people in that vicinity. Asahel, second son of Darius, fell a victim to his bravery and Indian barbarity. He was found killed and mutilated in the most shocking manner.

David Mead removed his family to Sunbury, where he commenced business as an innkeeper, and where he also erected a distillery. Shortly after the close of the Revolutionary War, he returned to his property in Wyoming County, thinking the disputes as to his title had ended. In this, however, he was greatly mistaken, and for three years more he contested the claim, but was finally compelled to vacate the property and go back to Sunbury. He was, on the tenth day of September, 1783, commissioned Justice of the Peace for the County of Northumberland.

Eli Mead, a brother of Darius, also settled in Northumberland County, and was appointed and commissioned a Justice of the Peace and also a Justice of the Court of Common Pleas for the District of Wyoming and County of Northumberland on the fourteenth day of July, 1786.

On the evening of May 12, 1788, a party of ten men built their camp-fire beneath a wild cherry tree on the banks of French Creek, near the present site of the Mercer Street Bridge, Meadville, Pennsylvania. They were the first settlers in Crawford County, and the party consisted of David Mead, his brothers, Darius, John, and Joseph, and others from Northumberland County, Pennsylvania. On the next day these pioneers built a cabin on the deserted corn fields of the Indians on the bottom, between the Cussewago and French Creeks, and commenced their first planting. David Mead first located west of the creek, designating his tract "Cussewago Island," and afterwards built a double log house on a bluff on French Creek, where is now the residence of Mr. James E. McFarland. This house was built with a view of defence against Indian attacks and was surrounded with a stockade fifteen feet high and protected by a small square log block-house on the northwest corner.

John Mead settled on the west side of the creek, north of the Cussewago Island survey, and Darius and Joseph settled in Warren County.

In the fall of 1788, the Mead settlers brought their wives and families from Northumberland County. In the David Mead house was the first white child born in Crawford County, his daughter Sarah, afterwards the wife of the Rev. Mr. Satterfield of Mercer County. Within two years David Mead built a sawmill on the north side of a deep precipitous ravine, then extending from the present property of Mr. James E. McFarland to the north side of the red mill. The power for this mill was supplied by a small stream long since gone.

During the year 1789 the little colony known as "Mead's Settlement" was reinforced by the arrival of other families. On April 1, 1791, the settlers were warned by Flying Cloud, a friendly Indian, of threatened danger from the hostile western tribes, and on the same day eleven strange Indians were seen a few miles northwest of the settlement. The women and children of the colony were gathered within the Mead house and on the next day sent in canoes to Fort Franklin. A friendly Indian chief, Half Town, was encamped here at the time with twenty-seven of his braves. Twelve of these he sent to guard the canoes, six on each side of the creek, and with his remaining warriors he joined the settlers in a fruitless search for the hostile tribes. On the following day all the men departed for Fort Franklin with their horses, cattle, and movable effects. On May third, a party consisting of Gregg, Ray, and Van Horne, returned to plant the spring crops. Stopping for the night at Gregg's cabin, they shelled a bag of corn, part of which they ground the next morning at the Mead house. Arriving at the corn field, Van Horne laid his gun on the bag of seed corn and ploughed, while Gregg and Ray planted. At noon Gregg and Ray returned to the Mead house for dinner and fresh horses. While ploughing, Van Horne saw two Indians emerge from the woods. The one dropping his bow and the other his gun, they rushed to the attack with their tomahawks. Van Horne grasped the uplifted arm of the first savage and entered on a struggle for his life. By his superior strength he shielded himself from the attack of his formidable foe with the body of his weaker antagonist, and called loudly for help. After a time the Indians promised his life on condition of surrender, which he did. Mounting the horses, Van Horne between them, they crossed the Cussewago Creek and entering a ravine on the hillside they met two other Indians. They then tied the hands of their prisoner and three of them returned to the corn field. Van Horne and the remaining Indian rode the horses to Conneaut Lake and crossed the outlet. Here they dismounted and Van Horne was tied by the ends of the rope, which secured his arms, to a tree, while his captor left in search of game. With a knife he had secreted he succeeded in cutting the rope and made his escape to the settlement, where by good fortune he found thirty soldiers under Ensign Jeffers on their return from Erie to Fort Franklin.

Gregg and Ray returning with the horses discovered the three Indians and fled, crossing the Cussewago Creek near its mouth. Gregg, after reaching the opposite bank, was wounded and while seated on a log he was shot by his pursuers through the head with his own gun. Ray was captured and carried to Detroit, then occupied by a British garrison. Here

The Family in Pennsylvania.

he was recognized by an old schoolmate of his boyhood in Scotland, Captain White, who purchased him from the Indians for two gallons of whiskey, furnished him with money and sent him on a vessel to Buffalo, from whence he was piloted to Fort Franklin by Stripe Neck, a friendly Indian, and soon afterwards he permanently settled in the northwest corner of Mead Township, Pennsylvania.

In the summer of the same year Darius Mead, the father, was captured near Fort Franklin by Captain Bull, a Delaware chief, in a field where he was at work, and carried to the vicinity of Conneaut Lake. Some days afterwards he was found with one of the Indians; both were dead, and bore marks of violence that showed that there had been a terrible struggle. It was thought probable that the other Indian had been severely wounded in the encounter, from the fact that he had left his companion unburied. They were buried side by side where found, near Shenango Creek, Mercer County.

The exposure of the frontier by the defeats of General Harmer, October, 1790, and General St. Clair, November, 1791, necessitated the abandonment of the settlement on French Creek during the greater part of 1791 and 1792. During the winter of those years the Mead house was garrisoned by a detachment of fifteen men from Fort Franklin. The command of the army in 1793 by General Wayne encouraged the return of settlers, who were for a time protected by a garrison of twenty-four soldiers under Ensign Lewis Bond; but the garrison was soon withdrawn, and the greater part of the settlers were compelled to return to Fort Franklin, and David Mead immediately wrote to Colonel Nevill, who had command of the forces on the frontier in that vicinity, as follows:

CUSSEWAUGO, July 11, 1793.

Sir:—We are just informed that the Federal troops at this station have been ordered to march in a few days down the

Ohio. Of course the post will be evacuated, and the settlement of the country much discouraged. Therefore, we request that you will be pleased to order a surjeant's command of State troops to support the Post. But should it not be in your power to grant us any relief, we wish you to let us know by the first opportunity what prospects we can have, and also that you forward the enclosed letter without delay.

I am, in behalf of the inhabitants, your most obedient and very humble servant,

DAVID MEAD.

Restored confidence, however, in 1794, added many new colonists, and substantial improvements were commenced. Law was in some degree enforced and a small company of militia was organized under the command of Ensign Van Horne. Indian alarms were not infrequent, and many times the Mead house gave refuge to the women and children from apprehended danger. The crushing defeat of the western Indians by General Wayne, August 20, 1794, restored safety to the frontier and many settlements were made on the navigable streams of Crawford County.

Previous to this David Mead had laid out the nucleus of the present city of Meadville, and had sold a few lots as early as February, 1793. In 1795 the town was resurveyed by David Mead and others, who had become interested with him. On June 3rd of this year occurred the last demonstration of Indian hostility in that County.

The first school was opened by Janet, daughter of Robert Finney, afterwards the second wife of David Mead, in 1795 in a log house on North Market Street. The following incident, which has been preserved by tradition, shows her strong character. In 1793 or 1794, William Gill took possession of and settled on the tract of land directly north of the Lord tract on French Creek. He built a cabin and raised corn and potatoes during the summer. In the fall he went to Pittsburgh, where his family were, intending to lay in supplies and return with his family. But, owing to the winter setting in early, he deferred his return until the following spring. When he arrived, he found the cabin occupied by Jenny Finney, who claimed possession of the land and stood in the door with rifle in hand and warned him to leave the premises; or, if he attempted to dispossess her, she would put a ball through him. Mr. Gill, believing discretion the better part of valor, abandoned the claim and went farther up the stream. Jenny Finney remained in possession long enough to perfect her claim, and in 1797 married David Mead, by whom she had six children. Perhaps the general could not have selected a more suitable companion. She was well educated, possessed a strong mind, an indomitable will and great energy of character. The tract of land settled by her finally became the property of her daughter, Maria, who married William Gill, the son of her mother's adversary in the land claim, and in the end, singularly enough, the descendants of the contending parties became joint owners of the property.

In 1796, David Mead received his patent from the commonwealth of Pennsylvania to his tract of land at Meadville, which is given as follows in the *Tribune-Republican*, Meadville, Pennsylvania, May 11, 1888:

THE COMMONWEALTH OF PENN'A.
TO ALL TO WHOM THESE PRESENTS SHALL COME, GREETING:

KNOW YE, That in consideration of the sum of forty-two pounds, seventeen and nine pence lawful money now paid by Daniel Meade into the Receiver General's Office of this Commonwealth there is granted by the said Commonwealth unto the said David Meade a certain tract of land called Meade Ville situate, including an improvement, on the West side of the River Ohio, Allegany and Connewango Creek, in Allegany County, BEGINNING at a black oak near French Creek, thence by land of Capt'n Jeffers, North seventy-five degrees, East four hundred and eight perches to a white oak, thence by land of Hugh Dupry, North one hundred and forty-four perches to a Post, thence by land of William Mead, South seventy-five degrees, West eighty-one perches to a Post, North forty-one perches to a Post, South seventy-five degrees, West two hundred and seventy-one perches to a Post at an Island, and thence down French Creek, by the several Courses thereof three hundred and twelve perches to the Beginning, containing four hundred and thirty-nine Acres, one hundred fifty-six perches and allowances of six per Cent for roads &c. Which said tract was surveyed in pursuance of an Act of the General Assembly passed the 3rd April, 1792, for William Mead, Who by Deed dated 1 January, 1796, conveyed the same to the said David Meade, to whom a warrant of acceptance issued the 12 January instant with the appurtenances. TO HAVE AND TO HOLD the said tract or parcel of land, with the appurtenances, unto the said David Meade and his Heirs to the use of him the said David Meade his Heirs and Assigns forever, free and clear of all restrictions and reservations as to Mines, Royalties, Quit-rents, or otherwise, excepting and reserving only the fifth part of all the Gold and Silver Ore for the use of this commonwealth to be delivered at the pitt's month clear of all charges.

IN WITNESS WHEREOF, Thomas Mifflin, Governor of the said commonwealth hath hereto set his hand, and caused the State Seal to be hereunto affixed the fifteenth day of January in the year of our Lord one thousand seven hundred and ninety-six, and of the commonwealth the twentieth.

ATTEST:
JAMES TRIMBLE,
Deputy Sec.

At the close of the century the village consisted in great part of log houses scattered on Dock, Water, Chestnut, Centre, and Walnut Streets. A few frame buildings had been erected, some of which remain to this day. The residence owned by Mrs. Byllsby on North Water and Market Streets was built for General David Mead in 1796.

Upon the organization of Crawford County, March 12, 1800, General David Mead was appointed one of the Associate Judges, but resigned the following December. In September, 1803, he was again appointed, and served continuously on the bench until the time of his death. During the Revolutionary

War he was 2nd Ensign, Colonel Hunter's Battalion, Captain John Simpson's Company, Associated Battalions and Militia of Pennsylvania. He was appointed Major-General of the Fourteenth, and afterwards of the Sixteenth Division Pennsylvania Militia, and during the War of 1812, rendered important services to Commodore Perry. In the summer of 1812, Captain Daniel Dobbins, of Erie, was sent by General David Mead to Washington as a bearer of dispatches, and was the first person who gave the Government reliable information of the loss of Mackinaw and Detroit. At his solicitation a naval station was established on the Lake and the construction of a fleet was immediately commenced. The command on the Lake was assigned to Lieutenant Oliver Hazard Perry, who arrived at Erie on the twenty-seventh day of March, 1813. His first step was to provide for the defence of the position. To that end he sent immediately for General David Mead, and their consultation resulted in a thousand militia being ordered to rendezvous at Erie on or before the twentieth day of April.

During the earlier stages of the construction of the fleet in the Bay of Presque Isle, considerable uneasiness was felt for fear the enemy would attack Erie and destroy the vessels before they were capable of making a defence. Commodore Perry urgently solicited General Mead to send a re-enforcement of militia to assist in defending the town, as he was expecting an attack. The general at once issued the following stirring appeal:

CITIZENS TO ARMS.

Your State is invaded. The enemy has arrived at Erie, threatening to destroy our navy and the town. His course, hitherto marked with rapine and fire wherever he touched our shore, must be arrested. The cries of infants and women, of the aged and infirm, the devoted victims of the enemy and his savage allies, call on you for defense and protection. Your honor, your property, your all, require you to march immediately to the scene of action. Arms and ammunition will be furnished to those who have none, at the place of rendezvous near to Erie, and every exertion will be made for your subsistence and accommodation. Your service to be useful must be rendered immediately. The delay of an hour may be fatal to your country, in securing the enemy in his plunder and favoring his escape.

DAVID MEAD, Maj. Gen., 16th D. P. M.

On the seventh day of August, 1813, the entire fleet was successfully launched. General Mead and staff visited Commodore Perry in the afternoon of the same day, and the latter took occasion to thank the commander of the land forces in the following letter, for the valuable assistance rendered him:

U. S. Sloop of War *Lawrence*,
Off Erie, August 7, 1813.

Sir:—

I beg leave to express to you the great obligation I consider myself under for the ready, prompt and efficient service rendered by the militia under your command, in assisting us in getting the squadron over the bar at the mouth of the harbor, and request you will accept, Sir, the assurance that I shall always recollect with pleasure the alacrity with which you repaired, with your division, to the defense of the public property at this place, on the prospect of an invasion.

With great respect I am, Sir,
Your obedient Servant,
O. H. PERRY.

Maj. Gen. DAVID MEAD,
Pennsylvania Militia, Erie.

On the twenty-second day of October, 1813, Commodore Perry wrote General Mead, as follows:

ERIE, October 22, 1813.

Dear Sir:—

It may be some satisfaction to you and your deserving corps, to be informed that you did not leave your harvest fields, in August last, for the defense of this place, without cause. Since the capture of Gen'l Proctor's baggage by Gen'l Harrison, it is

ascertained beyond doubt that an attack was at that time meditated on Erie; and the design was frustrated by the failure of Gen'l Vincent to furnish the number of troops promised and deemed necessary. I have the honor to be, dear sir,
Your obedient Servant,
O. H. PERRY.
Maj. Gen. DAVID MEAD,
Meadville.

In height General David Mead was head and shoulders above the average, being six feet three and a half inches, exceedingly well proportioned, of striking appearance and of great bodily strength. He died after a short illness, August 23, 1816.

CHAPTER VII.

THE FAMILY IN MILITARY AND CIVIL AFFAIRS DURING THE COLONIAL PERIOD.

WHILE Connecticut furnished more than her actual quota of men for active service in the different Colonial Wars, King William's War, 1689-1697, Queen Anne's War 1702-1713, and King George's War 1744-1748, still the author has been unable to find any record of any company, detachment, or squad of men having enlisted from Greenwich, nor any individual members of the Mead family, except as follows:

KING GEORGE'S WAR 1744-1748.

> JAMES MEAD, Ensign. The Assembly of June 19, 1746, resolved to raise one thousand men (including officers) for an expedition against Canada, and James Mead was appointed and commissioned to be Ensign of Captain Joseph Wooster's Company of Foot to be raised in Connecticut. This is the first record of any of the family in Connecticut or New York having served in the Army.

It is probable, however, that other members of the family were in active service during one or more of these wars, but as the original muster and pay rolls are still missing it is impossible to secure any authentic data with reference to their Connecticut war record during that time. It is hoped that the researches of future generations will bring to light all the original rolls.

THE FRENCH AND INDIAN WAR, 1754-1764.

The first muster and pay rolls that have been turned in and are now on file in the State Library at Hartford, Connecticut, are those of the French and Indian War, but as so many of them are missing it is impossible to obtain a complete list of those members of the family who were in active service during this war from the Colony of Connecticut. Connecticut was largely drawn upon for troops. Young men were pressed into the service, and as Greenwich, during the early part of the war, had no volunteer company, several of the inhabitants were pressed. James Green, now long since dead, used to relate that while a company of young people, himself among the number, were quietly enjoying themselves at the tavern, then kept by Henry Mead, they were surprised by a press-gang, and several of them forced into the service, while he with a few others escaped through a window. Soon after this a volunteer company was raised. This company under the command of Captain Thomas Hobby afterwards performed active service in the campaign of 1759 against Fort Ticonderoga and Crown Point in the 3rd Connecticut Regiment, Colonel David Wooster. The author has secured such names as he could find from the original muster and pay rolls, also from Hoadley's *Colonial Records of Connecticut*, and *Collections of the Historical Society of New York* for 1891, which are as follows:

CONNECTICUT FORCES.

1755.

Expedition against Crown Point.
French and Indians repulsed at Battle of Lake George,
September 9.

THADDEUS MEAD, of Norwalk, 2nd Lieutenant, 4th Company, 1st Regiment.

JOSEPH MEAD, of Greenwich, Corporal, Captain Thomas Hobby's Company. Enlisted September 11, discharged December 4.

GERSHOM MEAD, of Greenwich, Private, Captain Thomas Hobby's Company. Enlisted September 8, discharged December 24.

MATTHEW MEAD, of Norwalk, Private, Captain Samuel Hanford's Company. Enlisted September 8, discharged January 1, 1755.

1756.

Expedition against Canada, campaign ended without any engagement.

THADDEUS MEAD, of Norwalk, Commissary of the 3rd Regiment.

JAMES MEAD, of Greenwich, Private, Captain David Waterbury's Company. Enlisted April 21, discharged November 24.

1757.

Connecticut troops at Fort Edward.

CALEB MEAD, of Greenwich, Lieutenant, Captain White's Company, Colonel Jonathan Hart's Regiment.

JAMES MEAD, of Greenwich, Private, Captain David Waterbury's Company. Enlisted February 28. In the same Company last year.

1758.

Expedition against Crown Point and Fort Ticonderoga. Colonial forces repulsed at storming of the Fort.

THADDEUS MEAD, of Norwalk, 1st Lieutenant, 8th Company, 4th Regiment, Colonel David Wooster. Enlisted March 27, discharged November 13.

JAMES MEAD, of Greenwich, Ensign, 5th Company, 4th Regiment, Colonel David Wooster.

JOSEPH MEAD, of Greenwich, Ensign, 6th Company, 4th Regiment, Colonel David Wooster.

MATTHEW MEAD, of Norwalk, Quartermaster, 4th Regiment, Colonel David Wooster.

JOSHUA MEAD, of Norwalk, Private, Captain Archibald McNeil's Company, 4th Regiment. Enlisted April 19, discharged November 12.

GERSHOM MEAD, of Greenwich, Private, Captain Isaac Isaac's Company, 4th Regiment. Enlisted May 12, discharged October 30.

1759.

Expedition against Crown Point and Fort Ticonderoga.
Fort Ticonderoga evacuated July 27.

AMOS MEAD, of Greenwich, Surgeon, 3rd Regiment.

THADDEUS MEAD, of Norwalk, Captain, 9th Company, 3rd Regiment. Enlisted March 22, discharged December 3.

CAPTAIN HOBBY'S COMPANY OF GREENWICH.

JAMES MEAD, 2nd Lieutenant, 4th Company, 3rd Regiment. Enlisted March 22, discharged December 4.

JOSEPH MEAD, Ensign, 4th Company, 3rd Regiment. Enlisted March 22, discharged December 4.

SYLVANUS MEAD, Corporal, 4th Company, 3rd Regiment. Enlisted April 2, discharged December 5.

ELIPHALET MEAD, Private, 4th Company, 3rd Regiment. Enlisted April 2, discharged December 7.

JESSE MEAD, Private, 4th Company, 3rd Regiment. Enlisted April 16, discharged December 5.

CAPTAIN SAMUEL HUBBELL'S COMPANY.

JOSEPH MEAD, of Norwalk, Private, 3rd Regiment. Enlisted May 20, discharged December 3.

CAPTAIN ARCHIBALD MCNEIL'S COMPANY.

JOSEPH MEAD, of Norwalk, Private, 3rd Regiment. Enlisted April 15, discharged October 21.

1760.

Expedition against Montreal.

THADDEUS MEAD, of Norwalk, Captain, 10th Company, 3rd Regiment. Said to have been killed during this campaign, probably at the storming of Oswegatchie in August.

JAMES MEAD, of Greenwich, 2nd Lieutenant, 5th Company, 3rd Regiment, Colonel David Wooster. Killed.

JOSEPH MEAD, of Greenwich, Ensign, 5th Company, 3rd Regiment, Colonel David Wooster.

1761.

Expedition against the Indians.

MATTHEW MEAD, of Norwalk, Ensign, 12th Company, 2nd Regiment.

JOSIAH MEAD, of Greenwich, Private, Captain Thomas Hobby's Company. Enlisted April 6, discharged December 20.

JOSHUA MEAD, of Norwalk, Private, Captain Amos Hitchcock's Company. Enlisted April 7, served four weeks.

1762.

Expedition against Havana.

NOTE—Eleven Companies of the 1st Regiment, March, 1762, joined the expedition against Havana. The 10th Company of the 1st Regiment did not go, but served with the 2nd Regiment at Crown Point.

MATTHEW MEAD, of Norwalk, Ensign, 5th Company, 2nd Regiment. Enlisted July 15, discharged December 7.

JESSE MEAD, of Greenwich, Private, 5th Company, 2nd Regiment. Enlisted March 19, discharged December 7.

NEW YORK FORCES.

1755.

ZEBULON MEAD, 2nd Lieutenant, Captain Peter VanDenbergh's Company of Dutchess County.

1756.

ZEBULON MEAD, 2nd Lieutenant, Captain Peter VanDenbergh's Company of Dutchess County.

STEPHEN MEAD, Private, Captain VanDenbergh's Company of Dutchess County.

1758.

JOHN MEAD, Private, Captain Jonathan Ogden's Company of Westchester County.

1759.

GERSHOM MEAD, Private, Captain Jas. Holmes' Company of Westchester County. With the Connecticut forces in 1755 and 1758.

1760.

GERSHOM MEAD, Private, Captain Wm. Gillchrist's Company of Westchester County. Killed.
DANIEL MEAD, Private, Captain Jacobus Swartout's Company of Dutchess County.
LEWIS MEAD, Private, Captain Jacobus Swartout's Company of Dutchess County.

One of the descendants of Surgeon Amos Mead, the Hon. Seaman Mead, of Greenwich, Connecticut, has in his possession an old flintlock-pistol and powder horn, which were carried by him through the campaign of 1759, and upon the powder horn is almost perfectly delineated, the relative positions and forts of the hostile armies of Ticonderoga. This work was done by Dr. Mead while in active service as Surgeon of the 3rd Connecticut Regiment. The horn, besides, has engraved upon it the following:

"AMOS MEAD,
"Surgn of ye 3d Conn Reg
"Ticonderoga October 1759."

While there is no official record of the services rendered by Dr. Amos Mead, as Surgeon of ye 3rd Connecticut Regiment during the campaign of 1759, still the author has seen his original commission, which was duly issued under the Seal of the Colony of Connecticut and signed by the Governor. This document is also in the possession of the Hon. Seaman Mead. There is, also, no official record of the services rendered by Lieutenant Caleb Mead, of Greenwich, who served in Captain White's Company, Colonel Jonathan Hart's Regiment, in the campaign of 1757; but Mr. Walter C. Mead, of Denver, Colorado, son of the Hon. Cornelius Mead, of Greenwich, Connecticut, one of the descendants of Lieutenant Caleb Mead, has in his possession the original order of Colonel Jonathan Hart of the 9th Regiment to Lieutenant Caleb Mead, of which the following is a copy:

To Lieut. Caleb Mead, Lieut. of the Eaſtern Company in Horſeneck,

GREETING you are hereby ordered & commanded to march in perſon aſ Lieut. under Captain Stephen White at the head of the fourth part of the Company to which you belong which I have thiſ day ordered to march to the Relief & aſſiſtance of hiſ Majeſty'ſ forceſ & garriſonſ at fort Edward &c.

Given under my hand at Stamford thiſ 7th day of Auguſt, A.D., 1757.

(Signed) JONTH HART,
Colonel of ye 9 Regiment.

The following is a copy of the Commiſſion iſſued to Lieutenant Caleb Mead, May 29, 1745.

JONATHAN LAW, ESQ.:

Governour and Commander in Chief of Hiſ Majeſty'ſ Colony of Connecticut in New England.

To CALEB MEAD, Gent., GREETING:

You being by the General Aſſembly of thiſ Colony Accepted to be Lieutenant of the Eaſt Company or Train-band in the Town of Greenwich Repoſing ſpecial Truſt and Confidence in your Loyalty, Courage and good Conduct, I do by Virtue of the Letterſ Patentſ from the Crown of England to thiſ Corporation, me thereunto Enabling, Appoint and Impower you to take the ſaid Train-band into your Care and Charge aſ their Lieutenant carefully and diligently to diſcharge that Truſt; Exerciſing your Inferior Officerſ and Soldierſ in the uſe of their Armſ according to the Diſcipline of War; Keeping them in good Order and Government, and Commanding them to Obey you aſ their Lieutenant for hiſ Majeſty'ſ Service. And you are to obſerve all ſuch Orderſ & Directionſ aſ from time to time you ſhall receive either from Me or from other your Superiour Officer, purſuant to the Truſt hereby repoſed in you.

Given under my Hand and the Seal of thiſ Colony in Hartford the 29th day of May In the 18th Year of the Reign of Our Sovereign Lord GEORGE the Second, King of GREAT-BRITAIN, &c. Annoque Domini 1745.

(Signed) J. LAW.

By Hiſ Honour'ſ Command.
GEORGE WYLLYS, Secr.

THE FIRST BRICK HOUSE IN GREENWICH.
BUILT BY EPHRAIM MEAD IN 1820.

On March 2, 1756, it was voted "that Mr. Nehemiah Mead should have liberty to sell the Town stock of Powder as soon as he can conveniently to ye Towns best advantage and lay out all the money that he shall sell said powder for, in powder that is good and put the same into Town stock as soon as he conveniently can."

COMMISSIONED OFFICERS IN THE MILITIA FOR GREENWICH.

EBENEZER MEAD (2), 1728, May 9, was commissioned Lieutenant of the East Company, or train-band at Horseneck.
1738, May 11, was commissioned Captain of the same company.

SAMUEL MEAD, 1728, May 9, was commissioned Lieutenant of the West Company, or trainband at Horseneck.

JOHN MEAD (3), 1735, October 8, was commissioned Captain of the West Company, or trainband at Horseneck.

CALEB MEAD, 1745, May 29, was commissioned Lieutenant of the East Company, or trainband in the Town of Greenwich.

BENJAMIN MEAD, 1758, May 11, was commissioned Ensign of the West Company, or trainband in the Town of Greenwich.

BENJAMIN MEAD, JR., 1767, October 2, was commissioned Lieutenant of the new company, or trainband in the Town of Greenwich.

JOHN MEAD (4), General, 1757, October 13, was commissioned Lieutenant of the West Company of Greenwich.
1767, October 10, was commissioned Captain of the same company.
1774, October 13, was commissioned Major in the 9th Regiment.

MATTHEW MEAD, 1773, May 13, was commissioned Captain of the new company, or trainband of Greenwich.

ABRAHAM MEAD, JR., 1774, May 12, was commissioned Captain of the Middle Company, or trainband of Greenwich, 9th Regiment.

EBENEZER MEAD (4), 1774, October 13, was commissioned Ensign of the Middle Company, or trainband of Greenwich.

COMMISSIONED OFFICERS IN THE MILITIA FOR OTHER TOWNS.

NEHEMIAH MEAD, 1746, was commissioned Ensign of the 2nd Company, or trainband in the town of Norwalk. 1749, May 11, was commissioned Lieutenant of the same company.

STEPHEN MEAD, 1759, October 11, was commissioned Lieutenant of the Military Company in the Parish of Redding, 4th Regiment.
1767, May 11, was commissioned Captain of the company, or trainband in the west division of Redding Parish.

MATTHEW MEAD, 1773, May 13, was commissioned Captain of the company, or trainband in Wilton Parish in the Town of Norwalk.

JUSTICES OF THE PEACE FOR FAIRFIELD COUNTY.

EBENEZER MEAD (1), 1703, 1705 to 1709, 1714 to 1728 inclusive.
EBENEZER MEAD (2), 1733 to 1758 inclusive.
JABEZ MEAD, 1761.
JOHN MEAD (3), 1753 and 1754.
PETER MEAD, 1760 to 1774 inclusive.
STEPHEN MEAD, 1768 to 1770 inclusive.
JOHN MEAD (4), General, 1769 to 1774 inclusive.
AMOS MEAD, M.D., 1774.

SURVEYOR FOR FAIRFIELD COUNTY.

PETER MEAD, 1770, May 10, appointed by the Assembly.

DEPUTIES TO THE ASSEMBLY FOR GREENWICH.

JOSEPH MEAD, 1669 and 1671.
JOHN MEAD (1), 1679, 1680 and 1686.
JOHN MEAD (2), 1691.
EBENEZER MEAD (1), 1694, 1699, 1702 to 1704, 1709, 1711 to 1714, and 1716.
EBENEZER MEAD (2), 1733, 1734, 1737 and 1738.
BENJAMIN MEAD (1), 1725 and 1727.
JABEZ MEAD, 1738 to 1744, inclusive.
JOHN MEAD (3), 1741 to 1754, inclusive.
EBENEZER MEAD (3), 1744, 1745, 1747 and 1751.

JABEZ MEAD (Jr.), 1751, 1753, and 1765.
BENJAMIN MEAD (2), 1752, 1754, and 1755.
ELIPHALET MEAD, 1761.
PETER MEAD, 1774 and 1775.
JOHN MEAD (4), General, 1767 to 1775, inclusive.
AMOS MEAD M.D., 1770 to 1774, inclusive.

DEPUTIES TO THE ASSEMBLY FOR OTHER TOWNS.

SAMUEL MEAD, 1727, for Stamford.
NEHEMIAH MEAD, 1749, for Norwalk.
STEPHEN MEAD, 1768 to 1770, inclusive, for Redding.

SOME PROBATE MATTERS.

1703, October 14, the Assembly upon the request of Rachel Mead, widow and relict of Nathaniel Mead, late of the Town of Greenwich, deceased, granted "full power to Capt. Jonath. Sellick and Deacon Sam'll Hoyt to give legall conveyances of severall parcells of land, which the said Nathaniel Mead sold and alienated in his lifetime, but did not give deeds thereof, viz.: a small parcell of woodland of about eight acres and a halfe lying in the bounds of Greenwich and five roods of meadow lying in the bounds of Stamford; also his right in Coscob Neck: also ten acres of land exchanged by the said Nathaniel Mead for ten acres of land, which is inventoried to the estate of said Mead." The trustees refused to accept the trust reposed in them and the Assembly of October 13, 1709, appointed James Ferris, Jr., of Greenwich, "who hath marryed the said Rachel Mead, widow, to give legall and sufficient conveyances to the severall pieces of land aforementioned."

1727, October 12, Josiah Mead, as Administrator of James Ferris, petitioned the Assembly for permission to sell decedent's real property.

1734, October 10, Susannah Mead, as Administratrix of James Mead, late of Greenwich, petitioned the Assembly for permission to sell decedent's real property.

1757, October 13, Nehemiah Mead, of Norwalk, appointed to sell land of Amos Munrow, deceased, late of Ridgefield.

1760, May 10, Nathaniel Mead, petitioned the Assembly to sell land of Jonathan Fiske, deceased, late of Greenwich.

1761, May 12, Matthew Mead and Jeremiah Mead, of Norwalk, as Administrators of the Estate of Thaddeus Mead, petitioned the Assembly for permission to sell decedent's real property. This is said to be Captain Thaddeus Mead, of the 10th Company, 3rd Connecticut Regiment, who was killed during the campaign of 1760.

1763, May 12, Jemima Mead, as Administratrix of James Mead, deceased, late of Greenwich, petitioned the Assembly for permission to sell decedent's real property.

1771, May 9, Matthew Mead, of Norwalk, as Administrator of Betty Whelpley, deceased, petitioned the Assembly for permission to sell decedent's real property.

1772, May 14, Petition of Titus Mead and Sarah Mead, Executors of the will of Jabez Mead, who was Executor of the will of David Mead, to sell land of David Mead, deceased.

1772, May 14, Petition of Benjamin Mead, Jr., as Administrator of Gideon Mead, deceased, for permission to sell decedent's real property.

SOME LAW SUITS TAKEN ON APPEAL TO THE ASSEMBLY.

1751, October 9, Justus Bush vs. Nathaniel Mead, costs allowed respondent by the Assembly, £17 0s 0d. Old tenour.

1756, October 14, Nathaniel Barnum, of Danbury vs. Stephen Mead, of Fairfield. Action to partition land. Decision reserved by the Assembly and a new tryal ordered. Costs to abide the event.

1757, May 12, on petition of Stephen Mead and Samuel Close of Greenwich vs. Thomas Close. New tryal denied. Costs allowed respondent £4 15s 7d. Lawful money.

1763, May 12, on the petition of Gideon Reynolds vs. John Mead. Prayer denied. Costs allowed respondent £2 9s 8d.

1764, October 11, on the same as above vs. Jonas Mead. Petition denied. Costs allowed respondent £2 17s 9d. Lawful money.

1764, October 11, on petition of Josiah Mead, Executor of John Marshall, et al. vs. John Marshall, Jr. Costs allowed respondent £2 15s 4d. Lawful money.

1766, October 8, on petition of Josiah Mead of Greenwich vs. John Marshall and William Bush, Amos Mead and Ruth his wife, children and heirs of Justus Bush, deceased, late of Greenwich, praying for the recovery of certain real property.

CHAPTER VIII.

THE REVOLUTIONARY WAR.

THE Battle of Lexington, April 19, 1775, marks the beginning of that long and bloody struggle for American independence known as the Revolutionary War, during which, half of the hardships, privations and sufferings undergone by our ancestors, in defence and maintenance of their rights, has never been told.

At the outbreak of the war, some, from their loyal and religious zeal immediately sided with the enemy. However, they did not at that time openly avow their design. So little spirit was shown on the part of the tories within the limits of the town up to 1777, that a vote sustaining the Declaration of Independence, and the Continental Congress was passed in town meeting without a dissenting voice. Yet there were disaffected ones, as the event proved; and before the war was finished, ninety-two men, but none of the Mead family, had gone over to and openly joined the ranks of the enemy from the Second Society alone.

After the British had occupied New York, there arose another class of men, called cowboys, who were much worse than the tories. This body was composed of certain lawless characters, who seized upon every opportunity for plunder with avidity. They committed their depredations both upon the Americans and the enemy. Old grudges contracted before the war were now satisfied with relentless vigor, and the Americans suffered the most from these wretches. And inasmuch as they did by far the greater injury to the Americans, they were often assisted by British troops to carry out their nefarious designs. Skulking about at night in the woods and by-places, they would shoot down the inhabitants when they least suspected that an enemy was near. Their mode of warfare can only be compared with that of the Indians in the early history of the country. A few instances will show the bloodthirstiness which they had attained to about the close of the war.

Shubal Merritt, whose family is now extinct, was one of these. With one of his boon companions, he was lurking about the village of Rye, New York, for the accomplishment of some hidden purpose. An aged man was ploughing in a field near-by their hiding place, and as he diligently pursued his labors backward and forward across the lot, they were whiling away the time by playing cards. Finally, Shubal proposed a game to decide which should shoot the man. The result was against Shubal, who, as the old man approached them slowly with his team, deliberately raised his musket, and shot him through the heart. After the war was over, the murderer suffered his just deserts. A son of his victim met him and shot him dead upon the spot. And so great was the feeling of hatred to him on the part of the citizens, no notice was taken of the act.

Captain Sylvanus Mead, of Greenwich, Connecticut, a veteran of the French and Indian War, one of the Committee of Safety, and captain of a company of Rangers, was constantly watched and hounded by these wretches. They finally, during the early part of the year of 1780, traced him to the old Ralph Peck place at Mianus, Connecticut, and one of them knocked at the door. He called out from within "Who's there," when one of them answered by firing through the door. The ball

THE HOUSE IN WHICH CAPTAIN SYLVANUS MEAD WAS SHOT BY COWBOYS DURING THE REVOLUTIONARY WAR

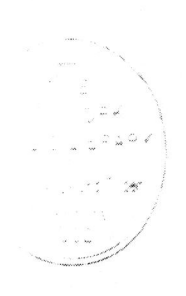

The Revolutionary War. 59

struck Captain Mead wounding him fatally, and he died the following day.

He was born January 19, 1739, and served in the French and Indian War as Corporal in Captain Hobby's Company, 3rd Connecticut Regiment, in the campaign of 1759 against Crown Point and Fort Ticonderoga. The enemy was compelled to vacate the fort on the 27th day of July. At the commencement of the Revolutionary War, he received a commission as Ensign in Captain Ebenezer Hill's Company, 7th Connecticut Regiment, Continental Line; was at the siege of Boston, and promoted to 1st Lieutenant, Captain Samuel Keeler's Company, Colonel Phillip B. Bradley's Battalion, Wadsworth Brigade, Connecticut State Troops, May, 1776. He was stationed during the greater part of the summer and early fall of 1776 at Bergen Heights (now Jersey City), and in October of that year was ordered up the river to the vicinity of Fort Lee, then under General Greene's command. In November most of the regiment, including Lieutenant Mead's Company, was sent across the river to assist in the defence of Fort Washington, which on the 16th day of November, 1776, was captured with its entire garrison, among whom was Lieutenant Mead. He was afterwards exchanged and promoted to captain of a company of Rangers raised by order of the Assembly of Connecticut, May 8, 1777.

He married, June 2, 1763, Sybil, daughter of Jonah Wood, of Huntington, Nassau Island, by whom he had Whitman, Platt, Gideon, and Asel.

Dr. Amos Mead, of Greenwich, Connecticut, who was ye Surgeon of ye 3rd Connecticut Regiment in the expedition against Crown Point and Ticonderoga in 1759, and also one of the Committee of Safety, was so chased and hunted by these men as to be obliged to travel about back in the country for a whole winter. He retraced by night the tracks he had made by day, and then moving off a short distance in another direction, spent the night in the first sheltered place that could be found. In the early spring following the winter of 1780, he came down to look at a field of wheat growing some distance back of his house, but, on arriving at a certain point in the road, he turned back, for he was impressed with the idea that he must not go any farther, but how to account for the impression he knew not. A few days after a neighbor met him and told him that five men bent on taking his life were in that very wheat-field with their loaded muskets aimed at a certain point in the road where he must have passed had he proceeded. Dr. Mead, wisely acting on this timely warning, retired again into the country.

Benjamin Mead (2), the father of Captain Sylvanus, moved to Quaker Ridge (North Greenwich). He also had a son Benjamin (3), who kept the old homestead formerly occupied by Mr. Solomon S. Mead, but now by Dr. Fred Hyde, a descendant of Benjamin Mead. During the Revolutionary War the old place was raided by a party of British and tories. Obadiah, son of Benjamin (3), was then quite a lad. His sisters Anna and Phebe, who were younger, hid with their mother in the cellar of the old house as the redcoats marched up the road and their father and the older girls, Mary and Theodosia, barricaded the doors and windows, while Obadiah, the only son, solicitous for the cattle without, drove them into the barnyard and then beat a hasty retreat to a neighbor's barn. An unfriendly tory, knowing the fact, informed the British soldiers who surrounded the barn, threatening to set fire to it unless he came out. He, too brave to surrender, jumped from the barn and ran across the orchard towards the rocks above Dyspepsia Lane, but the British followed. Seeing that escape was impossible, Obadiah surrendered, only to be immediately fired at and instantly killed. The ball passed through his left arm and

OLD HOMESTEAD OF BENJAMIN MEAD (2).

entered his side. For several generations the place of his burial was a sacred spot to the members of the family, and now, though unknown, it is not forgotten in memory. The coat he wore, showing the bullet holes and blood stains, has been preserved all these years, and is now in the possession of Mr. Solomon S. Mead. After killing the son, the redcoats forced their way into the house, but unable to find the father, they departed, taking with them the horse and all the geese.

General John Mead's house was repeatedly plundered and his cattle driven off by the tories and cowboys, his buildings torn to pieces, fences burned, and the lives of his family endangered. So great were their nefarious designs against his family that he was eventually compelled to remove them to New Canaan, Connecticut. For his losses the State of Connecticut afterwards gave him a large tract of land in Ohio, then considered of little value, and at his death it was divided among his children.

There are two instances of those marauding expeditions which have been preserved by the family, as well as many other accounts of those dark days.

One morning while they were at breakfast with some of the general's friends, the house was surrounded by a party of the Tory Light Horse, and they barely had time to escape through the back door, but not unperceived by the enemy. One of the horsemen rode up and demanded of Anna, one of the general's daughters, then a girl of eighteen, who came to the door, where they were hid. She refused to give a satisfactory answer, when he declared with an oath that he would kill her, and aimed a blow at her head with his sword. She, however, dodged the blow, and his sword struck the door-casing, cutting it quite in two. This door-casing was visible as long as the house remained standing, and was a memento of the harshness of war. Finding that he could not intimidate her, he remounted his horse, rode into the house, placed his foot under the edge of the table and tipped it over, breaking the dishes. Confronting a large mirror, he dashed his sword against the glass and broke it into a thousand pieces, at the same time exclaiming, "there's Congress for you." General Mead's son, Alan, was at that time a very small boy, and he hid behind some evergreens in the fireplace. Being very much frightened by their wanton and boisterous conduct, he began to cry, when the same tory said to him, "stop your noise, or I will cut your head off." Anna always declared that she would remember that man, no matter where she should see him; and singular to relate, she did often see him in after years in churches and other places.

At another time, when the oldest son, John, who was Drum-Major in the army, was at home on parole, it being a very dry time and the well at the house having given out, Mary, another daughter, Anna's twin sister, went to a spring some distance from the house to rinse some clothes. While there she saw her brother John run from the back door in his shirt sleeves, through the orchard, to a thicket that had sprung up from the roots of a tree that had been cut down, and there conceal himself only a short distance from her. In a few moments she was surrounded by the British and Tory Light Horse, who demanded of her where her brother had fled to. When she re-refused to give the information, a horseman rode up to her, drew his sword and placing it at her breast, swore he would take her life in an instant if she did not reveal her brother's hiding-place. Her presence of mind did not forsake her, and she explained that she came out there early in the morning, had not been from there, and therefore under the circumstances could not know what had taken place at the house. She was finally successful in convincing him that she did not know, and thus saved her brother's life, although the place of his concealment was within sight, and almost within sound of their voices.

After the family removed to New Canaan, Connecticut, Anna became acquainted with and married John Eells of that place. He also had been a soldier, and was at Ridgefield when that place was burned. They had eight children, and removed to Walton, Delaware County, New York, where they both died at an advanced age.

Mary married Levi Hanford, also a resident of New Canaan, Connecticut. In the month of October, 1776, Levi enlisted in a troop of horse, under Captain Seth Seymour, whose duty it was to guard and protect the seacoast. On the night of March 13, 1777, he, together with twelve others of the troop, was detailed as a guard and stationed at South Norwalk, Connecticut, then called Old Well. It was very dark, the weather was inclement, and in consequence, the officers were negligent in their duties. During the night they were surrounded by the British and tories from Long Island, who came over in whaleboats, and the whole guard were taken prisoners, Levi among the rest, he being at that time but a mere boy, a little over seventeen years of age. The prisoners were conveyed across the Sound to Huntington, from there to Flushing, and thence to New York. Upon their arrival in that city they were placed in the old Sugar House prison in Crown, now Liberty Street, near the Old Dutch Church, which at that time was used as a riding school for the British Light Horse, but afterwards converted into, and until recently used as, the General City Post Office. Of those who were taken prisoners then, all died in prison, of smallpox, or other diseases, except two, Ebenezer Hoyt, and Levi Hanford, who lived to be exchanged. The old prison, which is now torn down, was a brown stone building, six stories high, but the stories were low, the windows small and deeply set, making it very dark and confined. It was originally built for a sugar refinery, and for a long time was used as such. A Mrs. Spicer, who resided in the city, took a deep and lively interest in the condition of the prisoners, and went almost daily to visit them in the prisons and hospitals.

It was in the year 1782, that Levi Hanford married Mary, General John Mead's daughter, and they remained in New Canaan, Connecticut, about twenty-five years. In 1808, they removed to Walton, Delaware County, New York, with their five sons and four daughters, taking possession of a large farm and a log house of ample accommodations and settled near Anna, Mary's twin sister. On the fifteenth day of September, 1847, Mrs. Hanford was laid at rest in the burying-ground at Walton. Her death was the first in her family.

In January, 1852, an advertisement appeared in the *Journal of Commerce*, a New York paper, stating that the advertiser, David Barker, Esq., had in his possession a cane made from one of the beams of the old Sugar House in Liberty Street, and calling upon any surviving sufferer from that old prison to send in his name, so that he might have the pleasure of presenting the relic to him as a support in his declining years. To this call only five responded, disclosing the melancholy fact that of those prisoners, only five remained alive. Each of these applicants sent in with his name a brief account of his imprisonment and sufferings. From these statements, it appeared that Levi Hanford was the youngest of the five when imprisoned, and had been confined the longest time. There being so many applicants for the cane, it was decided to leave the choice to be determined by lot, and the cane fell to Mr. Hanford. He was in his ninety-fourth year when he received it. So delighted was he with this souvenir of his early years, that he always kept it near him, occasionally exhibiting it to those who visited him, and cherished and preserved it until the day of his death. This cane is now in the possession of his son, Mr. William B. Hanford, of Franklin, Delaware County, New York. The cane itself is three feet, two inches long, about one inch in diameter, gold mounted, and bears the following inscription :

"Old Sugar House Cane.
D—— B——
to
L—— H——."

Among the most inveterate tories was a family by the name of Knapp, who lived on what is now known as the Tracy place, but none of that family is now living in Greenwich. One o, them, Timothy, had been paying his attentions with a view to marrying a daughter of Mr. Titus Mead, then living in an old house near the corner of Mead Avenue and North Street, and on her refusing his hand, he proudly told her, that she should yet speak to him, and he would in turn take no notice of her. This threat was verified in a more terrible way than he intended. Horses were the most valuable booty that the refugees could lay their hands on, and knowing that Mr. Mead kept a fine horse, which he every night led up the oaken stairs to his garret, Knapp with two of his brothers went to the house to take it. Mr. Mead had knowledge of their approach and stationed a man who was with him at a back window upstairs. It was at dusk, and when the three men had come to the door-step, after some words, Mr. Mead fired, the ball passing through the door and entering the heart of Timothy Knapp. Without waiting to see the result of the shot, his brothers ran off in an easterly direction; and at the same time the man stationed at the back window sprang out and ran with all his might. The remaining refugees, seeing him, and supposing it to be their brother, called out, "run, Tim, run," which made him run the faster. At last, the daughter, opening the door and seeing Timothy lying there, asked him if he were badly hurt, but he made no answer and it was found that he was dead. She had spoken to him, and he had taken no notice of her. On finding that he was dead, word was sent to his family that his body was lying as it fell on the door-step. They paid no attention to the messenger, and after the body had lain there for a considerable length of time, Mr. Mead buried it in a lot belonging to the Knapps, in a pair of bars, where they must have driven over it in going in and out. Afterwards the family took up the body and buried it close by the house where he was shot, and his bones still rest there. A line of willow trees now mark the spot, a little way south of the house.

Another class, not so violent in their individual conduct, but equally inimical in other respects, was composed of those who under guise of permits from the English, resided here without molestation from the enemy, and in return for this privilege, gave them sufficient and well-timed information of the doings of the Americans. There was quite a large number of this class scattered in different parts of the country; and we cannot but deplore the situation of our forefathers, thus situated with spies and tories in their midst and the enemy close at hand.

During the war a paper was published in the City of New York by one Rivington, called the *Rivington Press*. This paper was professedly and to all outward appearances devoted to the British cause. It was, however, afterwards known to have aided the Americans much, and it is said that it was under the control of General Washington himself. The hostile appearance of the sheet deceived the Americans as well as their enemies. About half a dozen Greenwich men resolved that the publication of the *Press* should be stopped, and they stole into the city, destroyed the printing-press, and bagged the type, which they brought off with them from the very midst of a watchful enemy. Messrs. Andrew and Peter Mead were the principal men of the expedition. It is said that they only of the company were able to carry the bags of type from the printing office to the street, and throw them across the backs of their horses. After the type was brought to Greenwich it was totally destroyed, except enough to print the names of the members of the company, which the veterans kept for a long time in memory of their exploit.

During the period that New York was occupied by the British, their vessels had almost complete command of the waters of Long Island Sound. There were, however, many daring men engaged in a sort of privateering against them, and among these were Captain Andrew Mead and Elnathan Close, of Greenwich, with quite a large company of men. They went upon their expeditions in whale-boats, which might easily be hidden in the smaller bays along the coast and glide through shallow water in escaping or attacking the enemy.

In one of their expeditions, they proceeded by night to Ferry Point and seized upon a small store vessel and brought her off with them. She was anchored in a small inlet known as Chimney Corner. The prize was so valuable a one, that the enemy pursued them with one of their sloops of war and anchored off Chimney Corner a short distance from the shore; but the people of Greenwich collected for the defence of the prize, and fired upon the sloop from behind a knoll with a six-pounder, which was the only large gun in the town. The first shot struck upon the vessel's deck and wounded a dog, as was supposed from his sudden yelping. Other shots were fired and replied to by the enemy's guns, but finding it impossible to retake the vessel or harm the people upon the shore, the British relinquished their efforts and sailed away. Captain Andrew Mead was wounded on this occasion in both arms. As they were boarding the vessel at Ferry Point, he being the first to leap on her deck, received two shots, one in each arm, from the marines on guard, who, as the approach had been so still, then perceived the attack for the first time. Although Captain Mead was wounded, Elnathan Close and his crew, who boarded the vessel from the opposite side, quickly overpowered the marines on the deck and the force below surrendered with but little resistance.

The winter of 1779-1780 was one of the severest on record during the war. The Sound was completely frozen over and a great amount of snow fell. During the month of January 1780, some dozen or twenty head of cattle, the most of which belonged to Jared Mead, of Greenwich, were driven off in haste by the cowboys towards New York. After much solicitation on the part of the owners, Messrs. Andrew Mead, Richard Mead, and Humphrey Denton, of Greenwich, Connecticut, consented to make the daring attempt to cross the enemy's lines and retake the cattle. There had been recently a rainstorm, which had frozen as it fell, rendering the roads extremely slippery and making a hard, sharp crust upon the snow. The pursuers, however, went upon the Sound with their horses and kept the ice as far as Mamaroneck, New York, and then taking the road could track the cattle by the blood which had trickled from the prods of the bayonets given them to force them along. At Mount Vernon, New York, they retook the cattle and were returning when they found that they were being pursued by a body of troops under the command of a lieutenant. Their horses were tired by their long and swift ride, and they soon knew that their only safety was in separation; and in that case even, one must be inevitably taken. Accordingly they left the cattle and fled separately in different directions. The enemy selected Richard Mead, pursued and took him prisoner. He was taken to New York and thrown into the famous Sugar House, where he remained for a period of six weeks until exchanged.

Richard Mead was the son of Dr. Amos Mead, of Greenwich, Connecticut, and when he was about to take to himself a Colonial dame, in 1798, to share his lot, his father built a house and gave it to him as a wedding gift. It was called

THE RESIDENCE OF THE LATE COLONEL THOMAS A. MEAD.

Dearfield, the "dear" being spelled with an "a," and its fame spread far and wide as being a delightful and magnificent home, which it really was, and one of the sights of those times, as well as it is of these. The immense button-ball tree, which stands directly in front of the house, is a landmark. There were three standing during the Revolutionary War, the other two nearer to where the Presbyterian Church now stands, but this is the only one now remaining as a relic of those stirring times. The old homestead, the residence of the late Thomas A. Mead, Colonel, 9th Regiment, Connecticut Militia, is on Putnam Avenue. It was visited by General Lafayette in 1824, and is now occupied by a granddaughter and a great-granddaughter of Richard Mead, and a great-great-granddaughter of Captain Sylvanus Mead.

There is another very important Revolutionary incident, which while it does not directly concern the family, it might be well to relate, and that is General Putnam's perilous ride. The author being familiar with the topography of the hill as it now is, and having heard traditional accounts of that famous ride, which have been transmitted from sire to son, has selected the one that seems to him to be the most accurate and reliable. It appeared in the *Greenwich Graphic*, of July 21, 1897, and by courtesy of the *Graphic*, is reprinted here.

The Connecticut Historical Collections, published by J. W. Barber in 1838, is perhaps the most complete and valuable history of Connecticut extant. In this work we find the following description of Putnam's Hill and the daring exploit of General Putnam, also General Putnam's official account of the skirmish at Horseneck:

Putnam's Hill is situated in West Greenwich, about five miles west from Stamford, on the main road to New York. This place is celebrated for the daring exploit of General Putnam, who descended this precipice when pursued by the British dragoons. The place is considerably altered in its appearance since the Revolutionary War, by a road being blasted through the rocks at the summit of the hill, and continued by a causeway to the valley below. A small Episcopal Church formerly stood on the brow of the hill, a few feet south of where the road is now cut through, and the road passed north, and after proceeding to a considerable distance, bent again with a sharp angle to the south. The members of the congregation who lived below the hill, in order to save the tedious circuit of going round in the road, when walking to the church, placed stepping stones, in number about seventy, at suitable distances, so that foot passengers could ascend the precipice, directly up to the church. On the left extends a range of trees from the bottom to the top of the hill. These trees now occupy the place where the steps or stairs were situated, few or no traces of which now remain.

On the approach of Governor Tryon to this place, with a force of about fifteen hundred men, General Putnam planted two iron field pieces by the meeting-house, without horses or drag ropes. Having fired his cannon several times, Putnam, perceiving the dragoons (supported by the infantry) about to charge, ordered his men, about one hundred and fifty in number, to provide for their safety, and secured his own by plunging down the precipice at full trot. The dragoons, who were but a sword's length from him, stopped short, for the declivity was so abrupt that they dared not follow, and before they could gain the valley, by going round the brow of the hill in the ordinary way, he was far beyond their reach. One shot, however, of the many fired at him, went through his hat as he was passing down the hill. It has been generally stated that Putnam rode directly down the steps, but those who saw him pass down the hill say that he took a zig-zag course, commencing at the barn north of the house and continuing south until

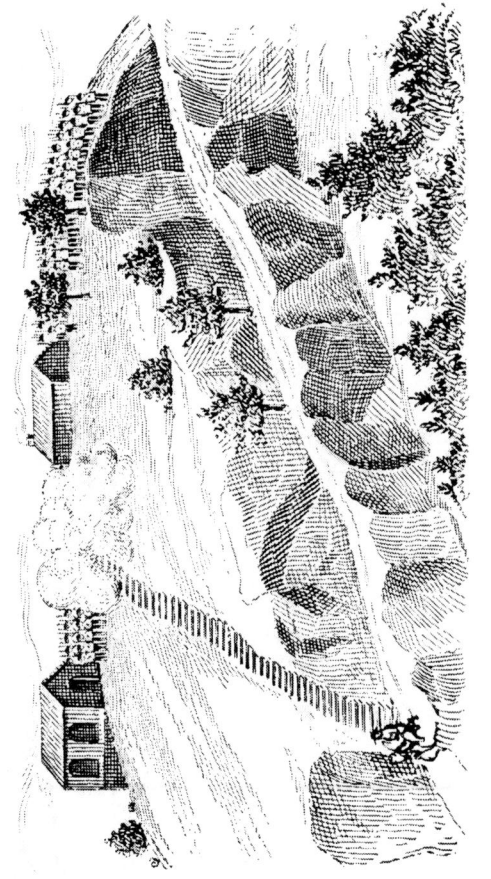

GENERAL PUTNAM'S RIDE.
FROM AN OLD SKETCH DRAWN BY GENERAL PUTNAM.
COURTESY OF THE "GREENWICH GRAPHIC."

he reached the steps, the lower ones of which he might have descended. This course would be sufficiently hazardous, and it is believed but very few men could be found who would dare make the attempt.

The following is General Putnam's official account of the skirmish at Horseneck:

CAMP AT READING,
March 2, 1779.

A detachment from the enemy at King's bridge, consisting of the 17th, 44th, and 57th British Regiments, one of the Hessians, and two of new levies, marched from their lines for Horseneck on the evening of the 25th ult., with an intention of surprising the troops at that place and destroying the salt works.

A captain and thirty men were sent from our advanced lines from Horseneck, who discovered the enemy at New Rochelle, in advance. They retired before them undiscovered, as far as Rye Neck, where, it growing light, the enemy observed and attacked them. They defended themselves as well as possible, and made their way good to Sawpits, where they took advantage of a commanding piece of ground and made some little stand, but the superior force of the enemy obliged them to retire over Byram bridge, which they took up, and by that means had an opportunity of reaching Horseneck in safety.

As I was there myself to see the situation of the guards, I had the troops formed on a hill by the meeting-house, ready to receive the enemy as they advanced. They came on briskly, and I soon discovered that their design was to turn our flanks and possess themselves of a defile in our rear, which would effectually prevent our retreat. I therefore ordered parties out on both flanks, with directions to give me information of their approach, that we might retire in season. In the meantime a column advanced up the main road, where the remainder of the troops (amounting to about sixty) were posted. We discharged some old field pieces which were there, a few times, and gave them a small fire of musketry, but without any considerable effect. The superior force of the enemy soon obliged our small detachment to abandon the place.

I therefore directed the troops to retire and form on a hill a little distance from Horseneck, while I proceeded to Stamford and collected a body of militia and a few Continental troops, which were there, with which I returned immediately, and found that the enemy (after plundering the inhabitants of the principal part of their effects, and destroying a few salt works, a small sloop and store), were on their return. The officer commanding the Continental troops stationed at Horseneck, mistook my orders and went much farther than I intended, so that he could not come up to them with any advantage. I, however, ordered the few troops that came from Stamford to pursue them, thinking they might have an opportunity to pick up some stragglers. In this I was not mistaken, as your Excellency will see by the enclosed list of prisoners. Besides these, eight or nine more were taken and sent off, so I cannot tell to which particular regiments they belonged; one ammunition and one baggage wagon were taken. In the former there were about two hundred rounds of canister, grape and round shot, suited to three pounders, some slow matches and about two hundred tubes; the latter was filled with plunder, which I had the satisfaction of restoring to the inhabitants from whom it was taken. As I have not yet got a return, I cannot tell exactly the number we lost, though I don't think more than ten soldiers, and about that number of inhabitants, but a few of which were in arms.

List of prisoners taken at Horseneck, the 26th ult.—17th Regiment, 15 privates; 44th do., 5 privates; 57th do., 3 privates; Loyal American Regiment, 5; Emmerick Corps, 8; First Battalion of Artillery, 1; Pioneers, 1.—Total 38.

N. B.—Seven deserters from Emmerick's Corps.

The following is an account of General Putnam's ride by Mr. I. L. Mead, the story having been related to him by his grandfather, Rev. Mark Mead, who received his information from Colonel Ebenezer Mead, who was standing in the dooryard of the house where John Maher now resides, and saw General Putnam as he rode down.

In those days there was no cut through the rocks, but the road ran north some distance, then turned in a southeasterly direction, using the old road as it now is half-way down the hill and crossing the present road going down on the south side. The road in some places was steep. On the top of the hill south of Putnam Avenue was the Episcopal Church. Pedestrians, instead of going around the road to the church, took

TRACY HOUSE.

the short cut up the hill. There were flat stones laid to give the people a better footing. When I was a boy there was a line of bushes where my grandfather told me the steps were. As near as I can remember, one corner of the building south of the present road stood on the line of steps. Anyone going on to the hill will see the impossibility of a horse going where these steps were, even at a walk and without a rider.

The story told in history with the picture of a man riding at full gallop down the steps, cut from immense stones brought from Voorhis' quarry, is on a par with many yarns that get into print. They are only fancy sketches of the writer.

There are various accounts given as to Putnam's movements before the enemy were discovered. Some say that he was at a ball the night previous, taking a lady on his horse behind him. The ball was near Peck's Land at the house standing where the William A. Husted house is. The lady was the daughter of David Bush, who lived in the house now occupied by Mr. E. P. Holly, of Cos Cob.

The Tracy house opposite the present Episcopal Church is claimed by some to have been the general's headquarters. Others say that his headquarters were at a house standing about opposite Mechanic Street, or Sherwood Place, as now called.

There was probably but a small force of men on duty here, and they were attacked by a much larger enemy. As soon as they caught sight of General Putnam they gave him full chase. He stopped to order his men to scatter. They did so, hiding behind trees and fences. Putnam started for the hill, and instead of going around the loop they were so close to him that he turned down a cow-path. This was too dangerous for the horsemen to follow. Anyone can locate this cow-path where General Putnam rode down if they will go where the old road joins the present road. By looking up towards Mrs. Button's house on the north side of the cut, you will see a natural pathway. It is very plain to be seen. This was at that time a cow-path. General Putnam could ride down there, but anyone would know it was dangerous. Anyone going on to the hill south of the present road must see that it would be impossible to get down there on a horse.

These conditions and the testimony of reliable witnesses (others saw it besides Colonel Ebenezer Mead and give the same account) convince me that this account of General Putnam's ride is the true one.

The above account given by Mr. I. L. Mead, practically agrees with the story about the ride told to the writer by Mr. Jabez Mead. His father related the facts to him, and said that that was what General Ebenezer Mead, who stood in his doorway, just beyond the foot of the hill told him about the ride. General Mead saw General Putnam come tearing down the cow-path; saw him turn in his saddle just as he reached the bottom of the stone steps and come into the turnpike, and holler "damn ye" to the redcoats who stood around the little church at the top of the steps, firing at him.—Editor *Graphic*.

CONTINENTAL LINE AND CONNECTICUT FORCES.
COMMISSIONED OFFICERS.

John Mead, of Greenwich, Brigadier-General
Matthew Mead, of Norwalk, Lieutenant-Colonel
Jasper Mead, Regimental Quartermaster
Abraham Mead, Captain   Matthew Mead, of Greenwich, Capt.
Caleb Mead, Captain   Sylvanus Mead, Captain
Jasper Mead, Lieutenant   Jehiel Mead, Lieutenant
Andrew Mead, Ensign   Jesse Mead, Ensign
Jeremiah Mead, Jr., Ensign

NON-COMMISSIONED OFFICERS.

Abraham Mead, Sergeant-Major   Nathaniel Mead, Sergeant
Azor Mead, Sergeant   Nemiah Mead, Sergeant
Caleb Mead, Sergeant   Peter Mead, Sergeant
Uriah Mead, Sergeant

Edmund Mead, Corporal   Halsey Mead, Corporal
          Libbeus Mead, Corporal
Uriah Mead, Fife Major, æ 80   John Mead, 3d Drum Major
Daniel Mead, Fifer   son of General John Mead
Oliver Mead, Fifer   David Mead, Drummer.
Samuel Mead, Fifer
Thespt. Mead, Fifer

PRIVATES.

Abel Mead	Isaac Mead	Nathaniel Mead, 3d
Abijah Mead	Israel Mead	Nemiah Mead, Jr.
Abraham Mead, 3d	Jacob Mead	Netus Mead
Benjamin Mead	James Mead	Obediah Mead
Calvin Mead	Jared Mead	Reuben Mead
Charles Mead	Jeremiah Mead, æ 85	Richard Mead
David Mead	Jespor Mead	Silas Mead, Jr.
Ebenezer Mead	Jesse Mead	Smith Mead, æ 80
Ebenezer Mead	John Mead	Solomon Mead
Elias Mead	Jonathan Mead	Stephen Mead
Elijah Mead	Jonah Mead	Thaddeus Mead
Elkanah Mead	Joseph Mead	Thaddeus Mead æ 76
Ely Mead	Josiah Mead	Theophilus Mead
Eneck Mead	Jothem Mead	Thomas Mead
Enoch Mead	Levi Mead	Titus Mead
Epenetus Mead	Lockwood Mead	Uriah Mead
Esben Mead	Matthew Mead	William Mead
Henary Mead	Nathan Mead	Zaccheus Mead.
Henry Mead, Jr.[1]		

CONTINENTAL LINE AND NEW YORK FORCES.

COMMISSIONED OFFICERS.

Hezekiah Mead, Captain   Job Mead, Captain
          Joel Mead, Captain
————Mead, Lieutenant   Nathaniel Mead, Lieutenant
William Mead, Surgeon   Enoch Mead, Adjutant
Jacob Mead, Ensign   Jehiel Mead, Ensign.

NON-COMMISSIONED OFFICERS.

Andrew Mead, Sergeant   Jonah Mead, Sergeant
Libbeus Mead, Sergeant   Isaiah Mead, Sergeant
Joshua Mead, Sergeant   Sely Mead, Sergeant.
Ezekiel Mead, Corporal   Halsey Mead, Corporal
Stephen Mead, Corporal   Joseph Mead, Drummer.

[1] Similar names are not duplications, but different individuals having the same name.

The Mead Family.

PRIVATES.

Aaron Mead	Israel Mead	Nathan Mead
Abner Mead	Israel Mead, Jr.	Nathaniel Mead
Abraham Mead	James Mead	Nehemiah Mead
Amos Mead	Jeremiah Mead	Noah Mead
Aron Mead	Jesse Mead	Paschel Mead
Bille Mead	Job Mead, Jr.	Richard Mead
Calvin Mead	Joel Mead	Selah Mead
Daniel Mead	John Mead	Silas Mead
David Mead	Jonathan Mead	Silas Mead, Jr.
Duncan Mead	Joseph Mead	Smith Mead
Ebenezer Mead	Josiah Mead	Thaddeus Mead
Edmund Mead	King Mead	William Mead
Edward Mead	Levi Mead	Zachariah Mead
Eli Mead	Louis Mead	Zalock Mead
Ethan Mead	Marsel Mead	Zebibediah Mead
Gilbert Mead	Marshall Mead	Zebulon Mead
Henry Mead	Marshel Mead	Zelek Mead.
Isaac Mead	Martial Mead	
Ismael Mead	Moses Mead	

CONTINENTAL LINE AND VERMONT FORCES.

COMMISSIONED OFFICERS.
James Mead, Colonel.

NON-COMMISSIONED OFFICERS.

Abner Mead, Sergeant	Abner Mead, Corporal
Jacob Mead, Corporal	Philip Mead, Corporal
Jacob Mead, Fifer	Truman Mead, Fifer.

PRIVATES.

Amos Mead	James Mead	Timothy Mead, Jr.
Benjamin Mead	Philip Mead	Timothy Mead, 3d
Ezra Mead	Rufus Mead	Truman Mead
Henry Mead	Stephen Mead	Zebulon Mead
Isaac Mead	Timothy Mead	Zebulon Mead, Jr.

In response to the first call for troops following the Battle of Lexington, April 19, 1775, quite a number of the family responded, entered the Continental Line, and participated in the Battle of Bunker Hill and the Assault on Quebec. During that year Connecticut had eight regiments in the field, five at Boston, and three in the Northern Division with forces from Vermont.

In addition to the large force of New York troops at the Battle of Long Island, August 27, 1776, Connecticut had in the field during that campaign eight Continental Regiments, and nine State Regiments, among this number was the 9th Regiment under the command of Lieutenant-Colonel John Mead, and upon an urgent request from the Commander-in-Chief for reinforcements, the militia consisting of fourteen regiments west of the Connecticut River and nine regiments east of the Connecticut River were ordered out. At New York these regiments were assigned to different posts and the brigade itself was divided with the militia into three or four brigades, one battalion of which was commanded by Lieutenant-Colonel Matthew Mead. The regiments saw much service during the summer and fall, some of them being engaged at the Battle of Long Island, the Retreat from New York, the Battle of Harlem Heights, the Battle of White Plains, and the Capture of Fort Washington. At the close of campaign a considerable number of the officers and men re-entered the Continental Line of 1777.

During the campaign of 1777, most of the troops were with the forces from New York and Vermont, and were at the Battle of Bennington and the Battles of Saratoga. The militia and remaining troops were engaged against Tryon in his raid upon Danbury, April 25-28, or in Meig's Sag Harbor Expedition, May 23.

The Campaigns of 1778-1781. The troops and militia, excepting the Continental Line, had many engagements in protecting the State from the numerous raids made by Tryon upon various towns, and Arnold's attack upon New London. The siege of Yorktown and the surrender of Lord Cornwallis, October 19, 1781, practically ended the war, although the Treaty of Peace was not signed until September 3, 1783.

Brigadier-General John Mead (4) was a direct descendent from the first John, through the oldest sons. His mother was Elizabeth Lockwood, of North Greenwich. He was born in Horseneck about 1725, died December 3, 1790, and was buried in the old burying ground at the summit of Put's Hill, but the spot is no longer known. In personal appearance he was short and very fleshy, so much so that a story is told of his tailor, who having made a vest for him, by way of experiment buttoned it around himself and four other men. In character he was extremely firm and decided, sometimes looked upon as a little severe, but, like all Meads, exceedingly just. He spent the whole of his life in Horseneck, having there a large farm. His residence was almost the first one in the village of Greenwich, entering it from the west, and was standing up to within a very few years. He was a member of the Legislature of Connecticut for eight years before the Revolutionary War, eight years during the Revolutionary War and after the Revolutionary War until 1788, two years before his death, making twenty consecutive years. He was Justice of the Peace for Fairfield County from 1769 to 1774 inclusive; commissioned Lieutenant of the West Company of Greenwich on the thirteenth day of October, 1757; promoted to Captain on the tenth day of October, 1767; and on the thirteenth day of May, 1773, received his commission as Major in the 9th Regiment, Connecticut Militia.

At the commencement of the Revolutionary War, King George sent him a commission as Captain, which he declined. He was commissioned Major when he entered the American Army; three weeks afterward was promoted to Lieutenant-Colonel, and three years before the war closed, was commissioned Brigadier-General. His Major's commission was at one time found by the British and tories among his papers, when they surrounded and plundered his house during the war, and by them carried off as evidence against him, should he by any chance of war fall into their hands. For three years during the war he had command of the American lines at Horseneck, and for a long distance each way. He saw much active service, served on the Brooklyn front with his regiment a few days before and during the Battle of Long Island, August 27, 1776, and in the retreat from New York had command of the last detachment of our troops that left the city. The day on which the troops evacuated New York was a remarkably hot one, and our men suffered intensely from that and fatigue during the retreat. At night, as soon as a place of safety had been reached, every one sought rest. The officers found accommodations on the floor of the hotel and elsewhere, till every place was occupied. Lieutenant-Colonel Mead came in last, carefully sought a place, and laid down, thoughtlessly appropriating an officer's feet for a pillow. The officer awoke, and in a rough tone demanded who was lying on his feet. Lieutenant-Colonel Mead politely apologized, but the officer recognizing his voice, cried out, "For God's sake, Colonel, is that you. I never expected to see you again alive after the dreadful heat and struggle of this day; make a pillow of my feet and welcome, if you can find any rest here." On September 15, he was posted on Harlem Heights and remained there until the Battle of White Plains, October 28, 1776, in which he was engaged and suffered considerable loss. He was afterwards posted at Horseneck and remained there during the greater part of the war, and took part in many other engagements. The sword that he carried through the war is in the posession of his grandson, Major Gabriel S. Mead, of Walton, New York.

General Mead was married in 1752, to Mary Brush, daughter of Benjamin Brush, of Scotch extraction. A tradition remains in that portion of the Brush family, to the effect that their descent is direct from Robert Bruce, and that on coming to this country the name was changed to Brush, to escape the possible notoriety that might be connected with the name. By this marriage he had nine children. His wife died in 1785, aged fifty-five. He married second, Mehetable, widow of Jonathan Peck and daughter of Mr. Blackman, of North Greenwich, Connecticut, and had one daughter, Mehetabel. He died December 3, 1790.

A few weeks prior to his death, however, General John Mead made and executed his last will and testament, which, from the following copy taken from the data collected by the late Rev. J. H. Hobart DeMille, it will be seen is quite lengthy and very explicit.

IN THE NAME OF GOD, AMEN, I, JOHN MEAD, of Greenwich in the County of Fairfield and State of Connecticut being sick and weak in body, but of a sound disposing mind and memory, thanks be to God for the same, and calling to mind that it is appointed for all men once to die and not knowing how short my time may be in this world do make and publish this last will & testament in manner following, and first of all I give up my soul to God that gave it hoping to receive salvation through the merits of my Saviour Jesus Christ, my body I commit to the earth to be decently buried with a Christian burial by my executors hereafter to be named, and as touching the goods and estate that it hath pleased God to endow me with I give and dispose of in the following manner.

FIRST, my will is that all my just debts and funeral charges shall be first paid out of my estate. Imprimis, I give unto my son John Mead the third of said Greenwich all my land Easterly of a line beginning at a heap of stones on the North part of my farm by the fence adjoining David Bushes land that was formerly Capt. Matthew Mead's and from thence running a strait line to the North End of the Burnt Swamp so called on the East side of said Burnt Swamp, until it meets the fence lately set up on the Easterly side of my wheat lot, where the wheat is now growing, Running South as said fence now stands by the bars top of Blind Garden Hill so called, thence running Easterly as the fence now stands North of said Blind Garden to Dr. Amos Mead land, called the great pasture, the whole of said tract of land is bounded Easterly and Southerly in part by Dr. Amos Mead's land & in part by the road leading from Horseneck to King St. Northerly in part by his own land and the land of David Bush & Westerly by the other part of my farm, which tract of land I give to my said Son John Mead the third, his heirs and assigns forever. Except what I may order to be sold out of said tract for the payment of my debts. I also give to my Son John Mead the third my old barn standing on my land at my field to improve it where it is or remove it on to his own land, I also give to my said Son John my old sorrel mare & a pair of three year old steers, one a yellow one, the other a black white faced one. Item, I give unto my other three sons and five daughters viz: Alan Mead, Seth Mead, Walter Mead, Mary Handford, Ann Eels, Elizabeth Hobby, Mary Ann Sniffen, and my little daughter Mehetabel Mead, the remainder of my land in the field so called. The said Mary Handford, Ann Eels, Elizabeth Hobby, & Mary Ann Sniffen deducting from each of their parts of said land what they have already had of my estate, except what may be ordered to be sold toward the payment of my debts, out of said tract of land which I reserve for that purpose. And I do hereby give Sd tract of land to said Alan, Seth, Walter, Mary, Ann, Elizabeth, Mary Ann, and Mehetabel to them, their heirs and assigns forever, the said Mary Handford, Ann Eels, Elizabeth Hobby, and Mary Ann Sniffen have deducted so much from their parts in said land as what they have already had out of my estate as above mentioned & my Sons, Alan, Seth, Walter, and Mehetabel will have so much more in said tract of land than an equal share as my other daughters have already had. Said tract of land is bounded Easterly by the land given to my Son John Mead, Northerly by the land of David Bush, Westerly by the lands of Abel Mather, Abraham Merritt & Cole Townsends lands & Southerly by the Blind Garden, so called, as the farm now stands, and I give liberty for my said children viz: the said Alan Mead, Seth Mead, Walter Mead, Mary Handford, Ann Eels, Elizabeth Hobby, Mary Ann Sniffen, & Mehetabel Mead to pass and repass as they may have occasion to & from their said land from the main country road, in the road or path where it now goes through the Blind Garden to their said lands, they doing no waste or spoil to anyone improving said Blind Garden. Item, I give unto my wife Mehetabel Mead the use & improvement of my dwelling house & barn standing on my home lot, also the use & improvement of my land

South of my Field commonly called Blind Garden containing about thirty five or thirty six acres in the whole and is the same land my father gave me with the house he bought of Peter How & the lands I bought of Dr. William Bush & Capt. John Grigg & is bounded Easterly by the road & fence leading through Sd Blind Garden with the equal half of the fence as it now stands against my son John's land & also the one half of the fence against my other heirs being the same line of fence. I also give to my said wife Mehetabel Mead the use & improvement of Alans, Seth, Walter, & my daughter Mehetabels parts until the said Alan, Seth, & Walter arrive to the age of twenty one years & the Sd Mehetabel to the age of Eighteen years to assist her in the supporting of my young children until the Sd Seth and Walter arrive at the age of fourteen years of age my will is they shall be put out to some proper trade by my executors hereafter to be named. What I have given as above to my said wife Mehetabel if she accepts the same in stead of her dower I give it her no longer than she shall remain my widow. If she shall marry again after my decease, or leave my said dwelling house & go elsewhere to live my will is that my Sd wife Mehetabel shall have the use and improvement of one third part of my said dwelling house & barn & also the use & improvement of one third part of all my real Estate during her natural life except such part of my real estate as may be found necessary to be sold toward the payment of my debts and no more. Item, I also give unto my three Sons Alan Mead, Seth Mead, & Walter Mead to them, their heirs and assigns forever, to be Equally divided between them after the decease of my said wife Mehetabel my said dwelling house & barn & about thirty five or thirty six acres of land in the same Blind Garden being the same house barn & lands that I have given my said wife Mehetabel the use of in lieu of her said dower and if either of said brothers viz: Alan Mead, Seth Mead, or Walter Mead shall die before they arrive to the age of twenty one years then the other one or two as the case may happen shall have his or their parts divided to him or them & not amongst the other heirs & farther my will is that if my daughter Mehetabel shall die before her marriage or before she shall arrive at the age of twenty one years then her part of my estate shall be Equally divided to and amongst the sisters & not amongst the sons. Item, I order my timber land lying in the Society of Stanwich East of Amos Mills dwelling house to be sold & the avails thereof to be applied to the payment of my debts. I also order my movable estate to be sold for the same purpose by my Executors hereafter to be named, except what I shall reserve for the use of my family & what by land & movable estate shall fall short in the payment of my debts my will that so much of my land be sold by my said Executors of my farm at Close's Field so called as will pay & settle the whole out of that part I have given to my son John & also out of the parts of the other heirs so as will do equal justice to the whole as nigh as may be. And I reserve out of my movable estate for the present use of my family two cows, my black mare, four swine, five sheep, one porridge pot, one dish kettle, one tea kettle, two cider hogsheads, one cedar washing tub, & four chairs, one trammel & the provisions that may be in the house for the use of my family only at the time of my decease, also one feather bed & furniture for the same.

Item, I give to my wife Mehetabel in the condition they may be in at the time of my decease all the household goods & furniture that is mine by virtue of my marriage with her that she brought to me & those that is in the hand of her son Jonathan Richard Peck provided she my said wife pay all his debts & costs that has arisen on the debts & now due against the estate of Jonathan Peck late of said Stamford dec'd on which estate she is administrator & also pay to Major John Davenport his fees as an attorney in the action brought against me by Frederic Whiting, Goal Keeper of Danbury, on account of her son Abraham Peck & if my said wife shall neglect to pay up the same agreeable to the average made out against said Estate & the cost that has arisen & still unpaid then my will is that so much of my household goods & furniture that is now in the hands of the said Jonathan Richard Peck & those she my said wife brought to me should be sold by my said Executors hereafter to be named as will fully satisfy the debts & costs aforesaid, which are as I suppose now in the hands of John Davenport, Esq., attorney &c., & the several articles above-mentioned that I have given for the present use of my family is to remain under the direction of my wife for the use of my said family, until the marriage or decease of my said wife & then to be sold for the use & benefit of my five daughters viz: Mary Handford, Ann Eels, Elizabeth Hobby, Mary Ann Sniffen, & Mehetabel Mead to be equally divided to and among them & their heirs and assigns forever & I do hereby nominate & appoint my wife Mehetabel Mead & my brother Nathaniel Mead of said Greenwich to be Executor of this last will & testament, revoking & making void all former wills by me made, ratifying, publishing & confirming this, and this only, to be my last will & testament.

In witness whereof I have hereunto set my hand & seal this 6th day of August Anno Domini 1790

JOHN MEAD

SIGNED SEALED PUBLISHED & DECLARED BY THE TESTATOR TO BE HIS LAST WILL & TESTAMENT IN OUR PRESENCE & HEARING

JOHN ADDINGTON
RICHARD MEAD
BEALE LEWIS

Colonel James Mead, of Vermont, born September 6, 1730, died January 17, 1805, was a direct descendant of the first John. His father was Timothy, who was the son of Jonathan, the fourth son of John (1). He was Colonel of the Vermont Militia during the Revolutionary War and served at Ticonderoga, June 29 to July 8, 1777; also in guarding the frontier, May 6 to 12, 1779. He married, August, 1752, Mercy Holmes, by whom he had Sarah, James, Abner, Samantha, Stephen, Mercy, Dorcas, Hannah, Damarius, Tameson, William, and James.

Lieutenant-Colonel Matthew Mead was a direct descendant of the first Joseph. His father was Jeremiah and his mother was Hannah St. John, of Norwalk, Connecticut. He was born in Norwalk, August 20, 1736, married February, 1760, Phebe Whelpley, and died February 26, 1816. He enlisted in the army, September 8, 1755, as private in Captain Samuel Hanford's Company, French and Indian War, served in the Expedition against Crown Point; in 1758 was commissioned Quarter master of the 4th Regiment in the Expedition against Crown Point and Ticonderoga; was commissioned and served as Ensign of the 12th Company, 2nd Regiment, in the Expedition against the Indians in 1761, and in 1762 as Ensign of the 5th Company, 2nd Regiment, in the Expedition against Crown Point. After the termination of the French and Indian War, he was on the thirteenth day of May, 1773, commissioned captain of the company, or trainband, in Wilton Parish in the Town of Norwalk, Connecticut Militia. At the outbreak of

PUT'S HILL IN 1895.

THE X ON THE RIGHT SHOWS THE PLACE WHERE GENERAL PUTNAM STARTED DOWN THE ROCKY STEEP.

the Revolutionary War, he received a commission as Captain in the 5th Regiment of Connecticut, Continental Line, was engaged in the Assault on Quebec in 1775, and wounded at St. Johns, Canada, on the sixteenth day of September, 1775. During the campaign of 1776, he served as Major in Colonel Stillman's Regiment, Connecticut State troops and Continental Line, and was in several engagements. The following year, 1777, he was Lieutenant-Colonel of the 5th Regiment of Connecticut, Continental Line, and in the engagement at Danbury during Tryon's raid, and in the Battle of Germantown, October 4. In the spring of 1778, he had command of the 8th Regiment of Connecticut, Continental Line. He resigned his commission May 25, 1778 after the winter of 1777-1778, at Valley Forge, where he was quartered with his Regiment.

The following is a copy of a letter sent by Thaddeus Mead to his father, Thaddeus Mead, of New Fairfield, Connecticut.

CAMP BEDFORD, New Purchase, Oct. 1, 1780.

HONOURED PARENTS :—

I with pleasure sit down to enclose a few lines to you, but time will not permit me to write every particular. I hope these lines may find you in a good state of health; they leave me so at present, through kind Providence. Perhaps you may think not so well of me for not writing to you, when I had an opportunity to send home a letter, but something would prevent. I should have sent a letter by Lieut. Hubbell, but did not know that he was going home till the morning before he set out for home. I was employed with making out returns till the moment he went. I have no news at present, only that we have been wonderfully preserved from the cruel enemy, by taking a spy, which brought the plan to light, which was laid between that treacherous General Arnold, and the British Officer. Had not that spy been taken, we should every one have been numbered with the dead, or prisoners, for we were on our march to West Point; but the wicked plan fell through, Blessed be God for the same. The spy had the plan of the fort, and all the works there, the number of men, the whole account of the regiments, ours likewise. I soon expect we shall move back to Horseneck; there is an Express gone from the Governor to General Washington to get orders to move back, we expect every hour that we will return. If you get settled down I will get a furlough if possible, but for fear I should not get a furlough I would not have you delay sending me some things, which I stand in need of now, shoes, stockings, breeches, shirts, mittens, and a handkerchief, for I can't get one down here, and I will reward you well. I cannot as yet expect to see you for tho I have petitioned in a manner for my audience of leave, yet I cannot obtain it, wherefore let me entreat of you to bear with me till such times as it lies in my power to make an honourable retreat, and then I shall not fail to hasten with the greatest celerity imaginable and give you an account of my entertainment, and of the recreation I have had in these parts. Till when, I subscribe myself, with a hearty presentation of my duty to my Parents and my love and respects unto all my other friends and relatives.

I am your obedient Son,

THAD. MEAD.

P. S.

I am in want of money. If you can send me a little as soon as may be, I shall be over glad. I should be very glad if you would come down and see me, for giving directions where to come I can't, for we will soon move from this place.

T. M.

DEPUTIES TO THE ASSEMBLY DURING THE REVOLUTIONARY WAR.

PETER MEAD, of Greenwich, 1775.
JOHN MEAD (4) General, of Greenwich, 1775 to 1783.
AMOS MEAD M. D., of Greenwich, 1775 to 1781.
BENJAMIN MEAD, of Greenwich, 1778.
MATTHEW MEAD, Colonel, of Norwalk, 1779.

CHAPTER IX.

THE WAR OF 1812.

WAR was declared, June 1812, and in the spring of 1813, Commodore Hardy, with a British fleet appeared off the eastern end of Long Island Sound, and for a length of time had almost complete control of the waters of the sound. Many vessels were burned or sunk by the enemy, and they pushed through the sound nearly to Throgg's Neck.

At this time the people of Greenwich and vicinity were greatly alarmed, and feared the enemy would attempt to land. The Pot-pie Company of Horseneck was posted on Field Point; the Cos Cob Company on Captain Noah Mead's Point, and a company from North Stamford on Greenwich Point. Mr. Bush Mead, one of the Horseneck Company, having been sent from Field Point after some straw, found on being challenged by the sentinel on his return, that he had forgotten the pass-word, and finally stammered out in reply, "Straw, straw for beds."

Mr. Selah Mead, one of the sentinels on Field Point, seeing but little excitement arising from the approach of the enemy, put into execution a practical joke of his own. Equipping himself in his birthday suit, he slipped without noise into the water, and swam silently around the point, where he found another sentinel asleep, whom he suddenly clasped around the waist, and shook to wakefulness, who awoke the neighborhood with his cries, supposing he was in the power of a real, live mermaid. Soon after this the enemy's ships withdrew to the eastern part of the sound, and the several companies were dismissed from guard duty. In case of alarm, however, the bells were to be rung, and one fine morning shortly after, the greatest consternation was created by the fierce ringing of the alarm-bells. Men hurried to and fro, and the news spread that the British had landed on Greenwich Point during the night, and the people, especially in Old Greenwich, were in a terrible flurry. The militia was hastily summoned and Major Ebenezer Mead, Jr., having collected his forces at Horseneck, hastened to the scene of action. Arriving at the meeting-house in Old Greenwich, about two miles from the position known to be occupied by the supposed enemy, he came to a halt and called for volunteers to reconnoiter. Mr. Whitman Mead, a son of Captain Sylvanus Mead of the French and Indian and the Revolutionary Wars, was the only one there who had courage enough to volunteer. Carrying a white handkerchief fastened to a cane he started off, and on investigation found the supposed enemy to be a fleet of American gun-boats under Commodore Lewis, who had been in search of one of the enemy's privateers, and had landed upon the point for breakfast. Mr. Mead so liked the joke that he stayed with the Commodore much longer than he should have done, and breakfasted with him. In the meantime our forces were in the greatest anxiety of suspense, and supposed that their scout had been taken prisoner and their flag of truce violated. He, however, returned safely and explained all to the officers of our forces, and they thereupon dismissed the troops and returned home. The Treaty of Peace of December 24, 1814, ended the war, and the Battle of New Orleans was fought, January 8, 1815, before notice of the termination of hostilities had been received.

Other members of the family, also, as official records show, served from Connecticut, New York, and Vermont, as follows:

The War of 1812.

REGULARS AND CONNECTICUT FORCES.

COMMISSIONED OFFICERS.

Ebenezer Mead, Jr., Major.   Seth Mead, Captain.

NON-COMMISSIONED OFFICERS.

Edmund Mead, Sergeant.   Bush Mead, Corporal.
Leander Mead, Sergeant.   Henry Mead, Corporal.
Bush Mead, Musician.

PRIVATES.

Jabez Mead,   Job Mead,   Rogers Mead,   Selah Mead.
James Mead,   Luke Mead, Samuel Mead,

VERMONT VOLUNTEERS.

COMMISSIONED OFFICERS.

Ezra Mead, Ensign.

NON-COMMISSIONED OFFICERS.

Josiah Mead, Sergeant.   Rufus Mead, Jr., Sergeant.

PRIVATES.

Elisha Mead,   Joel Mead,   Thomas Mead, Jr.,
Helon Mead,   Martin Mead, William Mead.
Henry Mead,   Samuel Mead,

NEW YORK VOLUNTEERS.

COMMISSIONED OFFICERS.

Thompson Mead, Lieutenant-Colonel, Commanding.
Enos Mead, Major.
Augustus Mead, Quartermaster-Sergeant.
Michael Mead, Captain.   Orison Mead, Captain.
Hiram Mead, Ensign.

NON-COMMISSIONED OFFICERS.

Ezekiel Mead, Sergeant.   Tyler Mead, Corporal.
Jesse H. Mead, Sergeant.   Israel Mead, Corporal.
Obadiah Mead, Sergeant.   Jacob Mead, Corporal.
William B. Mead, Sergeant.   Shadrach F. Mead, Corporal.
Ezbun Mead, Corporal.   William Mead, Corporal.

PRIVATES.

Abraham Mead,
Abraham Mead,
Abraham B. Mead,
Allen Mead,
Allen Mead,
Amasa Mead,
Artemus Mead,
Beckman Mead,
Daniel A. Mead,
David P. Mead,
Eber Mead,
Eber Mead,
Eber Mead,
Edward Mead,
Edward Mead,
Enos Mead,
Enos Mead,
Edmund W. Mead,
Ezekiel Mead,
George Mead,
Harvey Mead,
Henry Mead, Jr.,
Isaac Mead,
Isaac Mead,
Isaac Mead, Jr.,
James Mead,
James Mead,
James Mead,
James Mead,
James Mead,
James Mead,
James H. Mead,
Jeremiah Mead,
Jeremiah Mead,
Jeudethan Mead,
Jonathan Mead (seaman),
John Mead,
John Mead,
John Mead,
John Mead,
John Mead,
John Mead,
John Mead,
John P. Mead,
Joseph E. Mead,
Jotham Mead,
Levi Mead,
Lewis Mead,
Lewis Mead,
Lewis Mead,
Martin Mead,
Nathaniel Mead,
Nathaniel Mead,
Peter Mead,
Peter Mead,
Philip Mead,
Ralph Mead,
Samuel Mead,
Samuel Mead, Jr.,
Shadrach Mead,
Smith Mead,
Smith Mead,
Smith Mead,
States M. Mead,
Solomon Mead,
Stephen Mead,
Sylvanus Mead,
Tyler Mead,
Walter H. Mead,
William Mead,
William Mead,
William C. Mead,
William R. Mead,
Zalmuna Mead,
Zadock Mead (name also appears as Zodoc and Zadee).

Major-General David Mead, born January 17, 1752, was a descendant of the first John through the Jonathan branch. His father, Darius, was born in Horseneck, (Greenwich), Connecticut, March 8, 1718; removed from there to Nine Partners, Dutchess County, New York; thence to Hudson, New York; thence to Northumberland County, Pennsylvania, and thence to Crawford County, Pennsylvania, where he permanently settled. His military record is contained in Chapter VI.

Lieutenant-Colonel Thompson Mead, born February 26, 1774, was a descendant of the first John through the Jonathan branch. His father, Jonathan, who was born in Horseneck

MAJOR-GENERAL EBENEZER MEAD,
CONNECTICUT MILITIA.

about 1727, removed from there to Nine Partners, Dutchess County, New York, and thence to Chenango County, where he permanently settled. At the commencement of the War of 1812, the 17th Regiment, New York Militia, Lieutenant-Colonel Thompson Mead, Commanding, was ordered out on the first day of September, 1812, and participated in the Battle of Queenstown Heights.

Colonel Mead, married, February 26, 1795, Miriam Haight, by whom he had Julia, Allen, Almira, Thompson, Anson, Eliza, Clinton, Sarah, and Thompson, 2d. He was for many years Sheriff of Chenango County, New York.

Major-General Ebenezer Mead (4), of the Connecticut Militia, a direct descendant from the first John through the Ebenezer branch, was born December 12, 1748, and died in 1818. He served during the Revolutionary War as a private in Captain Hobby's Company, Colonel John Mead's Regiment, and after the Revolutionary War gained distinction as a training master in the militia. He was Major in the Connecticut Militia during the War of 1812, and at the time of the British scare, caused by the appearance of a British fleet, under Commodore Hardy, off the eastern end of Long Island Sound, which had almost complete control of the sound to Throgg's Neck, he was detailed to guard the coast against an invasion of the enemy. He had his forces stationed at several of the most strategic points, and through his vigilance the enemy was unable to effect a landing and was finally compelled to withdraw its forces from the waters of the sound.

He married, April 6, 1769, Nancy, daughter of Eliphalet Mead, by whom he had Nancy, Hannah, Marilda, Ebenezer (5), Rheumah, Jabez, and Amy.

Joseph E. Mead, of the Joseph line, [1] William, [2] Joseph, [3] Joseph, [4] Israel, [5] John, [6] Joseph E., born June 12, 1796, when but seventeen years of age was drafted into the army, War of

1812. He enlisted afterwards, and just before the war closed, was sent with his regiment to Green Bay, Wisconsin, to guard the frontier against the incursions of the Indians. In those days that was a long distance from New York, and as he had been so long separated from his family, he had lost all traces of them in the various changes of residence which they made. When he was mustered out of service, he remained in the vicinity of Green Bay, cultivating a tract of land, and trafficking with the Indians, sometimes extending his travels into Illinois, and often visiting Fort Dearborn. This fort was situated on the Chicago River, near the lake, and was surrounded for miles by a low marshy country, apparently unfit for cultivation, but which is now occupied by the City of Chicago and its suburbs. Joseph E. lived to see a beautiful city rise up from the swamp, and ever loved to relate his adventures among the wilds of the Northwest, before the hand of civilization had wrought such marvelous changes. He never married, but lived near Green Bay until he was about sixty years of age. While there, two young men came from McHenry County, Illinois, who were acquainted with Thomas R. Mead and his brother Charles. Seeing a man in the tavern where they stopped who resembled those two, they opened conversation with him, and found his name to be Mead also. They inquired if he had relatives in Illinois. He replied, "Not that I know of." They then told him that they knew two men by the name of Mead, living there, Thomas R. and Charles, and that he bore a striking resemblance to them both. He said that formerly he had brothers of those names, but he had supposed them dead long ago, as he had heard nothing from them, or any of his family in years; but that if these men were his brothers, they would find that Charles had two fingers chopped off, which he had done when they were boys together, and that Thomas had a crooked finger. On their return, the young men made known their discovery to Thomas, who recognized in the description, his long lost brother, whom all had supposed dead. He wrote him a letter, and in a short time Joseph returned to his relatives, and spent the remainder of his life with his brother Thomas.

CHAPTER X.

THE WAR WITH MEXICO, 1846-1848.

THE principal causes which lead to the Mexican War were the annexation of Texas and the aggressive action of the United States Government against Mexico. The Battle of Palo Alto, May 8, 1846, marked the commencement of active hostilities, and on the 13th day of May, 1846, Congress passed an Act providing money and men. Quite a number of the family volunteered, but owing to the small number of men called for, only a few were able to enlist, as appears from official records. The Treaty of February 2, 1848, ended the war, and the Mexican Government ceded to the United States an immense territory in the Southwest and on the Pacific Coast.

REGULARS AND VOLUNTEERS FROM CONNECTICUT.

Franklin Mead, Co. D., 1st Artillery.

NEW YORK VOLUNTEERS.

The following communication from the War Department, Washington, D. C., dated November 28, 1899, explains itself:

It is shown by the records on file in this Department that one Nicholas Mead was a member of Company D., 1st New York Volunteers. Nothing has been found of record in this Department to show that any other person with surname of Mead was a member of any volunteer organization from the State of New York in the service of the United States during the war with Mexico.

THE RESIDENCE OF MILO MEAD.
BUILT IN 1798.

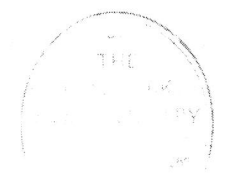

It seems that there are no records of the men who served during the Mexican War on file in the Adjutant General's Office at Albany, therefore the statement of the War Department has not been verified.

VERMONT.

During the month of September, 1899, the author received a communication from the Adjutant General's Office, Montpelier, stating that " we have no records of the Mexican War, but you can find those who served from Vermont in the War Department, Record and Pension Division, Washington, D. C."

In reply to a request for the information as to those who served, the War Department, Record and Pension Division, Washington, D. C., under date of November 28, 1899, advised "that there are no records on file in this Department of any volunteer organization from the State of Vermont in the service of the United States during the war with Mexico."

The fact nevertheless remains, notwithstanding these statements that the State of Vermont furnished her quota of volunteers for service in the Mexican War.

CHAPTER XI.

THE CIVIL WAR, 1861-1865.

THE bombardment of Fort Sumter, South Carolina, the first overt act by the seceded States against the Federal Government, began on Friday, April 12, 1861. The fort was surrendered by Major Anderson on the following day, after an attack in which one man was wounded, but none killed. The news was published in the papers of Sunday, April 14, 1861, and on Monday morning, April 15, 1861, President Lincoln's first proclamation, calling for 75,000 men to suppress the rebellion, was issued. This was followed, May 3, 1861, by an additional proclamation calling for forty more regiments and 18,000 seamen, and on July 2, 1862, by a call for 300,000 volunteers.

At the outbreak of the war, individual members of the family were aroused to a degree of enthusiasm and patriotism rarely witnessed even during the exciting times of those days, and many promptly responded to the first call for volunteers, and were early at the front both with commissions and in the ranks. The young men who enlisted were the flower of its manhood. They were representatives of the leading families and in their toilsome marches and battle scarred campaigns, they were nobly sustained by their people at home, who remained to furnish the "sinews of war."

Early in the war the women of the family allied themselves with soldiers aid societies, which were continued throughout

The Civil War, 1861-1865.

the conflict and proved of invaluable service to the objects of their solicitude. It was through their efforts that large sums of money were raised and valuable aid given to the Union cause. The reverses of the Union Army under McClellan in the early summer of 1862 only quickened their patriotic spirit, and during the entire conflict the family contributed both men and money liberally to the Union cause. Not only were there men at the front from Connecticut, New York, and Vermont, but also from the great West and Northwest, where members of the family had early settled, who were among the first pioneers of those wild and unknown regions and had made for themselves and their families new homes. In this and various other ways the family has become scattered, so much so that the author has found the task too difficult to include in this volume the names of those who served in the war from all the States or to relate the many deeds of heroic valor displayed on the field of battle by individual members of the family, or instances of sublime devotion to the Union cause of those who remained at home.

The surrender of General Lee April 9, 1865, ended the war.

CONNECTICUT VOLUNTEERS.

COMMISSIONED OFFICERS.

Daniel M. Mead, Major,
Thomas R. Mead, Captain,   David W. Mead, Lieutenant.

NON-COMMISSIONED OFFICERS.

George A. Mead, Sergeant,   John M. Mead, Corporal,
Zachariah Mead, Sergeant,   John D. Mead, Musician.

PRIVATES.

Aaron B. Mead,   Francis D. Mead,
Benjamin L. Mead,   Frederick Mead,
Charles L. Mead,   Hanford Mead,
Edward Mead,   Henry H. Mead,
Edward A. Mead,   Hibbard Mead,
Eliphalet Mead,   Isaac L. Mead,

James E. Mead,
Jeremiah O. Mead,
John D. Mead,
Ralph S. Mead,
Rufus Mead, Jr.,
Rufus N. Mead,
Silas E. Mead,
Smith Mead,
Ward B. Mead,
Watson N. Mead.

REGULAR AND VERMONT VOLUNTEERS.

COMMISSIONED OFFICERS.

John B. Mead, Colonel,
John B. T. Mead, Lieutenant.

NON-COMMISSIONED OFFICERS.

Egbert H. Mead, Sergeant, Charles B. Mead, Corporal,
George C. Mead, Sergeant, Charles E. Mead, Corporal,
C. Eugene Mead, Corporal, Darwin Mead, Wagoner,
Geo. D. Mead, Musician.

PRIVATES.

Cyrus H. Mead,
Ezra L. Mead,
Franklin Mead,
Franklin S. Mead,
Gardner C. Mead,
George Mead,
George A. Mead,
George E. Mead,
John A. Mead,
Morris D. Mead,
Royal Mead,
Wolcott A. Mead.

NEW YORK VOLUNTEERS.

COMMISSIONED OFFICERS.

Charles D. Mead, Division Judge Advocate, (Colonel),
Sidney Mead, Captain, William W. Mead, Captain,
Henry T. Mead, Adjutant, George W. Mead, Regimental Quartermaster,
Arthur J. Mead, Lieutenant,
Augustus W. Mead, Lieutenant, George U. Mead, Lieutenant,
Elias A. Mead, Lieutenant, John Mead, Lieutenant,
Joseph N. Mead, Lieutenant.

NON-COMMISSIONED OFFICERS.

Andrew J. Mead, Sergeant,
Charles Mead, Sergeant,
Wm. B. Mead, Sergeant,
Alvin Mead, Corporal,
Elnathan Mead, Corporal,
Fletcher Mead, Corporal,
Frank Mead, Corporal,
Isaac N. Mead, Corporal,
Judson Mead, Corporal,
John Mead, Blacksmith.

MAJOR DANIEL M. MEAD,
10TH REGIMENT CONNECTICUT VOLUNTEERS.

The Civil War, 1861–1865.

PRIVATES.

Abner B. Mead,
Absalom Mead,
Adolphus Mead,
Allen Mead,
Amzi Mead,
Asa C. Mead,
Asael Mead,
Austin Mead,
Charles Mead,
Cyrus Mead,
Daniel Mead,
Daniel Mead, Jr.,
Dryas H. Mead,
Dwight Mead,
Edward C. Mead,
Edward C. Mead,
Edwin F. Mead,
Elias Mead,
Frank C. Mead,
Frederick A. Mead,
George Mead,
George Mead,
George H. Mead,
George W. Mead,
George W. Mead,
George W. Mead,
Gideon Mead,
Henry Mead,
Henry H. Mead,
Henry W. Mead,
Jacob Mead,
James Mead,
James Mead,
James Mead,
James A. Mead,
James M. Mead,
James McF. Mead,
James P. Mead,
J. S. Mead,
James S. Mead,
Jeremiah Mead,
Jeremiah C. Mead,
John Mead,
John Mead,
John Mead,
John F. Mead,
Joseph Mead,
Joseph W. Mead,
Joshua Mead,
Lafayette Mead,
Lafayette Mead,
Lawrence Mead,
Lemuel D. Mead,
Lewis M. Mead, (Regular)
Lucius H. Mead,
Lyman Mead,
Martin Mead,
Napoleon Mead,
Nathaniel Mead,
Nelson H. Mead,
Norman Mead,
Oscar Mead,
Peter C. Mead,
Ransom H. Mead,
Seneca Mead,
Seth Mead,
Sidney M. Mead,
Stephen Mead,
Sylvester Mead,
Thadd Mead,
Thomas Mead,
Thomas G. Mead,
Volney Mead,
Walter F. Mead,
Walton Mead,
Warren Mead,
William Mead,
William A. Mead,
William H. Mead.

Major Daniel M. Mead, of the John line-Ebenezer branch, a descendant of Captain Isaac Howe of the Revolutionary War, was born in Greenwich, Connecticut, June 2, 1834. He attended Yale College and the Law School at Poughkeepsie, New York, was admitted to the Connecticut Bar, practised law at Horseneck, married June 16, 1856, Louisa S., daughter of the late Colonel Thomas A. Mead by whom he had no children, and in 1857, published *Mead's History of Greenwich, Connecticut.*

At the commencement of the Civil War, he enlisted, September 6, 1861, in the 10th Regiment Connecticut Volunteer

Infantry, as Captain of Company I., and on the fifth day of June, 1862, was promoted to Major, 10th Regiment Connecticut Volunteers, for gallant service. While at the front he was taken sick with typhoid fever and sent home, where he died September 19, 1862.

Captain Thomas R. Mead, of the John line-Ebenezer branch, a descendant of Dr. Amos Mead, Surgeon of ye 3d Connecticut Regiment, French and Indian War, and of Richard Mead of the Revolutionary War, was born in Greenwich, Connecticut, April 23, 1836. At the commencement of the Civil War, he enlisted, September 6, 1861, as Lieutenant in Company I, 10th Regiment Connecticut Volunteer Infantry, and later was promoted to Captain for gallant service. He died of typhoid fever at Washington, North Carolina, October 25, 1862, after thirty-seven weeks and four days of active service at the front.

The following is the history of the 10th Regiment Connecticut Volunteer Infantry as written by Brevet Brigadier-General John L. Otis, late Colonel of the regiment.

The 10th Regiment of Infantry was recruited late in the summer of 1861, mustered into the United States service September 30, at Camp Buckingham, Hartford, Connecticut, left there for Annapolis, Maryland, October 31, under command of Colonel Charles L. Russell, of Derby, and was assigned to the First (General J. G. Foster's) Brigade of Burnside's Division. The regiment remained at Annapolis two months, during which time it became noted for superior drill and discipline.

January 2, 1862, it took transports with the Burnside Expedition for North Carolina, remained on shipboard, miserably provided for, over five weeks; then landed February 7, and on the eight fought like a regiment of veterans in the Battle of Roanoke Island, losing fifty-six killed and wounded— the heaviest loss sustained by any regiment engaged. Colonel

CAPTAIN THOMAS R. MEAD,
COMPANY G, 10TH REGIMENT CONNECTICUT VOLUNTEERS

Russell was killed, and was succeeded by Colonel Albert W. Drake, of Windsor.

February 11, the regiment re-embarked and remained on transports over a month longer, landing at Slocum's Creek March 13, and after a hard day's march and a night bivouac in the mud again distinguished itself for steadiness and efficiency under fire on the morning of the fourteenth, in the Battle of Newbern, losing twenty-seven killed and wounded. Colonel Drake died June 5, and was succeeded by Colonel Ira W. Pettibone, of Winsted.

The 10th Regiment remained in North Carolina during the summer of 1862, taking part in all the movements of the Army. It was sent to Roanoke Island to suppress a mutiny, a battalion was sent to Plymouth to take part in capturing some rebel works on the Roanoke River, and the whole regiment took part in the Trenton and Tarboro expeditions, meeting the enemy at Rawle's Mills, Hamilton, and Williamstown. July 22, all troops in North Carolina were organized into the 9th Corps, under command of Major-General Burnside. November 15, Colonel Pettibone resigned, and the command of the regiment devolved for a short time upon Lieutenant-Colonel Pardee, and then on Lieutenant-Colonel Robert Leggett. December 14, 1862, during the Goldsboro Expedition, there was a very sharp engagement at Kingston, North Carolina. General French, of the rebel army, occupied the town with about 7,000 men; one of his brigades under Colonel Mallett occupied a strong position on the opposite side of the Neuse River, to defend the approach to the bridge. Several Union regiments had attempted to carry the enemy's position, but were all repulsed; the 10th Regiment was then sent for from the rear, passing, on its way to the front, one entire brigade and three regiments of another. Arriving in position, it charged the enemy over three regiments lying down in line of battle, drove the enemy from its position, pursued them to the Neuse River, charged and carried the bridge, which was on fire, and, swept by four guns in a *tete-du-pont*, captured five hundred prisoners, a like number of small arms, and eleven pieces of artillery, with a loss of one hundred and six killed and wounded. From the time the 10th Regiment commenced its charge, not a soldier of any other infantry regiment took part in the engagement. On the sixteenth the regiment took part in the engagement at Whitehall, and on the eighteenth, in that of Goldsboro. At this time Colonel T. G. Stevenson, 24th Massachusetts, commanded the brigade; General Foster, the expedition and the department. December 24, the troops then in North Carolina were, by order of the President, made to constitute the 18th Corps, with Major-General J. G. Foster in command.

January 29, 1863 General Foster led a division of his troops (of which Stevenson's Brigade, including the 10th Regiment formed a part) to South Carolina, for the purpose of making an attack on Morris Island and Charleston. Foster's troops were landed on St. Helena Island, where on February 13, Major John L. Otis of Manchester, was commissioned Colonel and assumed command of the regiment. Before leaving the island the regiment established its well-earned reputation of being the best drilled and best disciplined of any troops in the service. While here General Forster, with thirty men from the 10th Regiment made a complete reconnoissance of Morris Island, and declared it in a condition to be easily captured by a small force. But difficulties with Hunter and his staff, arising from childish jealousies on their part, resulted in Foster's return to Newbern, leaving Stevenson's Brigade behind, which was soon after assigned to General O. S. Ferry's Division of the 10th Corps. April 9, 1863, the brigade left St. Helena Island for Edisto Inlet, and on the next day the

10th Regiment landed under the guns of Commodore Rogers' monitor and drove the enemy from Seabrook Island, losing one killed and two wounded. While stationed on this island, the regiment was ordered to make a reconnoissance on John's Island, out of reach of support from the main body. The enemy had taken up the planking of the bridge connecting the two islands, and had a good force of infantry, artillery, and cavalry stationed so as to prevent relaying it. Colonel Otis, having but a single regiment of infantry with him retired to a good position and sent back for another regiment of infantry and a section of artillery. Meantime the enemy crossed to Seabrook Island with the hope of capturing the 10th Regiment before reenforcements could arrive; but they arrived in season and the enemy was attacked with such vigor that they were driven from the island in confusion, pulling up the bridge planking after them.

On July 14, Stevenson's Brigade took transports for James Island, landed there on the sixteenth, and became a part of Ferry's Division, 10th Corps. On the seventeenth the enemy drove the 54th Massachusetts from its position, where it was holding one of the causeways, marched five regiments of infantry, a battery, and a squadron of cavalry on the island, and unwittingly formed their line of battle so that it left the 10th Regiment on their right and rear. As our main line of battle outnumbered them two to one, and faced them at not more than two hundred and fifty yards distance, Colonel Otis begged permission to attack their right and rear while at this disadvantage, but permission was peremptorily refused. The two lines of battle faced each other for a few minutes without a shot being fired, then the enemy faced to the right, marched deliberately past our front, and off over one of the causeways, without molestation.

Colonel Otis was ordered to " follow them up closely, but in no case to bring on an action." This he did capturing several prisoners. There is no doubt that every rebel soldier who came on the island would have been killed or captured had an attack been ordered. On the morning of the eighteenth Ferry's Division marched across Cole's Island to a position opposite Folly Island, and after several hours' delay took transports for Morris Island—the whole brigade arriving just in time to form the third column of attack on Fort Wagner; but the order to charge was countermanded just as the brigade came under fire. Next morning Chaplain Trumbull and Adjutant Camp, understanding that a truce had been agreed upon, went out among the wounded, and inadvertently getting within the enemy's lines, were captured and taken to Charleston. Two weeks later Colonel Otis was detailed for special duty, and Lieutenant-Colonel Leggett having been severely wounded, the command of the regiment devolved temporarily upon Major E. S. Greeley, of New Haven. Although the regiment suffered but little loss on the Morris Island, its service there was ardous and trying. The courage and soldierly qualities of both officers and men were severely tested; they were constantly on duty, and at the front every third day, exposed to the fire of all the rebel fortifications about Charleston. When ordered to St. Augustine, after the capture of Fort Wagner, sixty per cent. of the men were on sick list.

In November Colonel Otis was relieved from special duty, resumed command of the regiment, and was placed in command of the Post and District of St. Augustine. While stationed here a force of the enemy's cavalry one hundred and sixty strong ambushed a detail of about thirty-five wood-choppers from the 10th, commanded by an officer from another regiment; the officer and two men were killed and twenty-one captured.

April 18, 1864, the regiment took transports for Virginia, reported at Gloucester Point the twenty-fifth, and was assigned to the Third Brigade, Ferry's (First) Division, 10th Corps, Army of the James. This army was composed of the 10th Corps under General Gillmore, and the Eighteenth Corps under General Smith, the whole under command of General B. F. Butler.

On May 7, the regiment took a conspicuous part in the affair at Port Walthall Junction, driving the enemy away from the railroad and destroying the telegraph, while other troops tore up the track. General Plaister the brigade commander, who had never before seen the 10th Regiment under fire, expressed astonishment and admiration at its matchless steadiness in action. May 13, 14, and 15, the regiment took an active part in all the preliminary movements and skirmishing preceding the Battle of Drewry's Bluff, and on the sixteenth was conspicuous throughout the day in that engagement. The right flank of the 18th Corps should have rested on the James River, but "through somebody's blunder," it did not, and the enemy marched a force between that flank and the river, capturing two brigades and leaving the right in such condition that the 10th Corps, which was forcing back the enemy's right, was ordered to withdraw and send re-enforcements to the 18th Corps. To the 10th Regiment was assigned the duty of holding the enemy in check while Hawley's Brigade on its right and Pond's on the left withdrew from the front; a duty which rendered the regiment liable to be overwhelmed and captured by the heavy force sent against it. Here again it won the applause of many officers of rank who witnessed its conduct, holding the enemy in check until the other troops had gained a safe position, then retiring in perfect order, halting twice to drive back the pursuing forces. The brigade commander said of this affair in his official report:

Of the 10th C. V., I need hardly say more than that they fully sustained the splendid reputation they have hitherto borne. For steady and soldierly behavior under most trying circumstances . . . . they may have been equalled, but never surpassed. Under a fire in which eighteen fell from the left of the regiment in almost as many seconds, not a man spoke a word or moved a heel from the alignment.

The moment this duty had been accomplished the regiment was sent to the front farther to the right, with orders to hold the enemy in check there until other troops could gain a safe position; this accomplished, Colonel Otis was ordered to take his own and another regiment of infantry, with a section of artillery, advance to the Half-Way House, and hold a position there on the Richmond and Petersburg pike until the last of the 18th Corps had passed to the rear. The enemy, with both infantry and artillery, attempted to force the position, but failed completely. The 10th Regiment was then sent far out to the right of our retreating army to protect its flank, and remained there until all had passed to the rear, then became the rear-guard back to Bermuda Hundred. In these movements the regiment lost thirty-six killed and wounded—none missing, although at three different times during the sixteenth it had been in danger of capture through holding its ground so tenaciously while the corps was retiring.

Early in June the regiment took part in repelling the attack of Beauregard on the Bermuda Hundred lines, when Major-General Walker of the rebel army was wounded, and captured; Beauregard himself barely escaped. June 15, the 10th Regiment was on duty at the front near Wier Bottom Church, Major Greeley in command. About three o'clock in the morning signs of a movement on the part of the enemy were observed. A skirmish line soon demonstrated that the enemy was retiring, on which the main body of the regiment advanced so rapidly as to capture, without loss, the famous Howlett House Battery, with thirty men and two officers. On the evening of June 20, a division under General Ferry moved down to Jones' Landing, on the James River, with orders to cross by a pontoon bridge and capture Deep Bottom, a position north of the James, and only nine miles from Richmond. There was so much delay with the pontoons that the general, fearing daylight would reveal and defeat the movement before the bridge could be completed, ordered Colonel Otis to select another infantry regiment in addition to his own, cross the river in boats, and capture the position. The 11th Maine was selected in addition to the 10th Connecticut the movement promptly executed, and the position captured at two o'clock in the morning. At daylight the enemy appeared in force with infantry and artillery to retake it, but were promptly repulsed. From this time to the end of the war Deep Bottom was the base of operations against Richmond. A few days later two detachments were sent out from the regiment to go within the enemy's lines, capture and destroy a gristmill with a large amount of grain, and also capture a torpedo station and bring away the apparatus. Both expeditions were completely successful.

August 10, the regiment was on duty at the front. The enemy made determined attacks on the line and were repulsed with considerable loss. The 10th Regiment being well protected, lost but one killed and three wounded. The following correspondence between Generals Butler and Foster, relative to the affair, speaks for itself—no other troops than the 10th Regiment were engaged:

>Headquarters Third Brigade, First Division,
>   10th Corps, Army of the James,
>   Deep Bottom, Va., August 1, 1864.
>Colonel J. L. Otis, Commanding 10th C. V.:
>   Sir:—I have the honor to forward the following dispatch from Colonel J. W. Shafter, Chief-of-Staff, in answer to a dispatch in relation to the affair in which your regiment was engaged this afternoon.

The dispatch by telegraph from General Butler's Headquarters. August 1, 1864.
General Foster:
Your dispatch is received. The Commanding General thanks you and your troops for the gallant manner in which you repulsed the attack on your lines this evening.
(Signed) J. W. Shafter, Colonel and Chief-of-Staff.
Very respectfully, your obedient servant,
P. A. Davis, Capt. and A. A. G.

July 26, Colonel Otis was again ordered to take the 10th Connecticut and the 11th Maine, cross from Deep Bottom to Strawberry Plains, and retake a position from which a brigade of the 19th Corps had been driven the evening before. The two regiments recovered the position, forced the enemy back into their intrenchments, and held a position within fifty yards of their works through the night. In the morning the two regiments joined a brigade of the 2nd Corps in charging the works; the 10th Connecticut and the 11th Maine carried an angle of the works, capturing three field guns. Loss of the 10th Connecticut, nine killed and wounded. August 17, Lieutenant-Colonel Leggett, being too much disabled by wounds received on Morris Island to continue in the field, resigned and was succeeded by Major Greeley.

August 26, the regiment fought with its usual gallantry and steadiness in forcing the enemy's lines in front of Deep Bottom and Spring Hill, losing thirty-six killed and wounded. Two days later, with the 24th Massachusetts and 100th New York, all under command of Colonel Otis, it took the advance in moving against the enemy at Deep Gully and Fuzzell's Mills, losing thirty-two killed and wounded. In short, the 10th Connecticut was in all of the nameless and almost numberless fights and skirmishes of the Army of the James during the summer of 1864. August 28, the regiment was ordered into the lines at Petersburg, where it remained thirty days, and although no serious engagement took place there during the time, it suffered a loss of nineteen killed and wounded, having been under fire night and day the whole time.

September 26, the regiment returned to the north bank of the James, and on the twenty-seventh took part in the engagement at Chapin's Farm, which resulted in the capture of Fort Harrison and Newmarket Heights.

October 1, General Birney found that the enemy was moving in force northward across the front of the 10th Corps, became alarmed for the safety of a body of troops under General Ferry that had been moved so far to the right as to become disconnected from the main body, and ordered the 10th Regiment to advance without support and attack the marching column of the enemy. The regiment advanced so promptly that it took a force of the enemy's cavalry by surprise and sent it flying from the field; then advancing rapidly, attacked the main body of the enemy in flank, compelling them to halt and form in line of battle facing the woods from which their cavalry and pickets had been driven. The 10th Regiment, by changing position rapidly in the woods, gave the rebels the impression that they were attacked by a much heavier force, which kept them stationary until Ferry's safety was assured. General Birney personally thanked the regiment for the pluck and coolness it had displayed in attacking and keeping inactive for two hours a force that outnumbered it ten to one.

September 30, the three years' term of the regiment expired. Losses in battle, by disease, and the muster-out of the non-reënlisted men reduced the command to but little more than one hundred men present for duty. October 7, when Kautz's Cavalry was stampeded without making a fight, and Lee's Army came down to drive the Army of the James back across the river, the regiment on the right of the 10th Connecticut broke and ran, leaving the 10th Connecticut on the extreme right of the army, where it was attacked by a rebel brigade pushed forward to turn our flank; the regiment stood its ground and drove back the entire brigade in confusion. The enemy rallied and again advanced, and was driven back the second time with heavy loss, leaving their dead, including three regimental commanders, on the field. The loss of the 10th Regiment was eight killed and wounded. General Plaisted said of this affair in his official report: "In my opinion, the conduct of the 10th Regiment, when the troops on its right broke and fled, saved the Army of the James from disaster."

October 13, the regiment, with but ninety men in the ranks, was ordered to join Pond's Brigade in charging a heavy and well-manned line of intrenchments on the Darby Road, five miles from Richmond. The force sent in was entirely inadequate and met with a bloody repulse, the 10th Regiment losing forty-six killed and wounded—just one more than half the number taken into the fight. The enemy was not only thoroughly intrenched, but outnumbered the assaulting column five to one. During the service of more than three years, this was the first time the regiment had fallen back under fire.

October 18, Colonel Otis was mustered out by reason of "expiration of term of service," and the command of the regiment devolved upon Colonel E. S. Greeley, of New Haven. October 28, the 10th Regiment under his command, had a sharp skirmish near the Gerhardt plantation with the loss of five wounded, and near the Johnson place on the twenty-seventh with one wounded. The following week the 10th Connecticut was one of the regiments selected to go to New York City and preserve order there during the Presidential election.

In November and December the regiment was recruited with

substitutes up to about eight hundred men. March 28, 1865, Colonel Greeley being absent on leave, the regiment, under command of Lieutenant-Colonel E. D. S. Goodyear, broke camp north of the James, with orders to march to the extreme left of the lines south of Petersburg. It reached Dinwiddie on the evening of the twenty-ninth; on the thirty-first took post at Hatcher's Run, and the next morning at four o'clock was attacked by a brigade of North Carolina troops, which it whipped handsomely, taking a number of prisoners. April 2, four companies being on picket, Lieutenant-Colonel Goodyear was ordered to take the other six and join in the assault on Fort Gregg, a key to the inner defences of Petersburg. After a march of over three hours he joined the assaulting column, which had to advance under the fire of Forts Gregg, Bradley, and Cemetery Hill. The fighting for a foothold on the parapet of the fort was desperate, and continued for more than half an hour with the bayonet and clubbed muskets. The 10th Regiment carried the southern angle of the works, and its State flag, with twenty-three bullet holes through it and three through the staff, was the first banner planted on the parapet. The desperate character of the combat is shown by the losses sustained; out of thirteen officers and one hundred and eighty men of the 10th Regiment that were engaged, eight officers and one hundred and eighteen were killed or wounded. The corps commander, General Gibbons, presented to the regiment a bronze eagle in recognition of its services on the occasion. General Grant himself gave the order for the charge, and in his *Memoirs* speaks in high terms of the conduct of the troops engaged. Lieutenant-Colonel Goodyear was severely wounded in the charge, and the command of the regiment devolved upon Captain Hickerson, under whom it marched in the van of the infantry sent to support Sheridan. Lee's plan was to defeat the cavalry and escape around the flank of the Army of the Potomac. He had already broken through the cavalry when the infantry of the 24th Corps, after a march of almost unprecedented hardship, formed across his line of march, barring effectually his further progress. Sabers alone, as Sheridan had foreseen, could not stop Lee's strong infantry column, but the bayonets of the 10th and the 18th Corps (the old Army of the James), combined in the new 24th, proved an impassable barrier. The rebels advanced on the infantry and some sharp fighting took place, during which the 10th Regiment had several men wounded and seven captured. The prisoners all escaped and got back during the day, but thoroughly cleaned out of everything valuable.

The regiment remained at Appomattox until the last rebel had been paroled, leaving there on the fifteenth day of April. On the sixteenth Colonel Greeley resumed command of the regiment, which moved deliberately "On to Richmond," where it remained until August 26, when it was ordered home and was mustered out of service at Hartford, Connecticut, September 5, 1865 — four years, lacking twenty-five days.

PRINCIPAL ENGAGEMENTS.

Roanoke Island, N. C., Feb. 8, 1862.
Newbern, N. C., Mch. 14, 1862.
Kinston, N. C., Dec. 14, 1862.
Whitehall, N. C., Dec. 16, 1862.
Goldsboro, N. C., Dec. 18, 1862.
Seabrook Island, S. C., Mch. 28, 1863.
Siege of Charleston, S. C., from July 28 to Oct. 25, 1863.
St. Augustine, Fla., Dec. 30, 1863.
Walthall Junction, Va., May 7, 1864.
Drewry's Bluff, Va., May 13 to 17 (inclusive), 1864.
Bermuda Hundred, Va., June 16, 1864.
Deep Bottom, Va., June 20, 1864.
Strawberry Plains, Va., July 26 and 27, 1864.
Deep Bottom, Va., Aug. 1, 1864.
Deep Bottom, Va., Aug. 14, 1864.
Deep Run, Va., Aug. 16, 1864.
Deep Gully and Fuzzell's Mills, Va., Aug. 28, 1864.

The Civil War, 1861-1865.

Siege of Petersburg, Va., Aug. 28 to Sept. 29, 1864.
Fort Harrison, Va., Sept. 27, 1864.
Laurel Hill Church, Va., Oct. 1, 1864.
Newmarket Road, Va., Oct. 7, 1864.
Darbytown Road, Va., Oct. 13, 1864.
Darbytown Road, Va., Oct. 27, 1864.
Johnson's Plantation, Va., Oct. 29, 1864.
Hatcher's Run, Va., Mch. 29 and 30, and Apl. 1, 1865.
Fort Gregg, Va., Apl. 2, 1865.
Appomattox Court House, Va., Apl. 9, 1865.

CHAPTER XII.

THE SPANISH-AMERICAN WAR, 1898.

ON the night of February 15, 1898, the United States Battleship *Maine*, while lying peacefully at anchor in the harbor of Havana, Cuba, was destroyed by an explosion. The following morning the entire country was aroused by the startling message from Captain Sigsbee, "*Maine* blown up, suspend judgment." The officials at Washington took immediate action, a Court of Inquiry was appointed and sent to Havana to ascertain, if possible, the cause. The country waited in suspense the report of that Court, which on the twenty-fifth day of March, 1898, was delivered to the President, on the twenty-eighth of March, transmitted to Congress, and " in the opinion of the Court the *Maine* was destroyed by the explosion of a submarine mine." Reparation was demanded by the Government, but refused, and on the twenty-second day of April, 1898, a proclamation was issued by the President declaring war. This was followed on the next day by a proclamation calling for 125,000 volunteers. The greatest enthusiasm and patriotism were shown throughout the entire length and breadth of the land. Many members of the Mead family volunteered, and enlisted in the provisional regiments, which were organized for the purpose of going to the front, among the number the author, but the quota of each State was so small that only a small proportion of those eager to go were mustered into the United States service. The campaign was short and decisive. The Protocol signed on the twelfth day of August, 1898, ended hostilities, and the Treaty of Peace was signed at Paris, on the tenth day of December, 1898.

CONNECTICUT VOLUNTEERS.

Harry A. Mead, Musician,
Seaman M. Mead, Private,
Harry A. Mead, re-enlisted for service in the Philippines.

VERMONT VOLUNTEERS.

Charles W. Mead, a descendant of the Vermont family, served as 1st Lieutenant, Montana Volunteers. After the close of the war he re-entered the service with a commission as captain in the 36th Infantry, United States Volunteers, and was sent with his regiment to the Philippine Islands. Brevetted Major for valiant service and afterwards appointed Engineer to the United States Philippine Commission.

George W. Mead, Private,
Robert P. Mead, "
William H. Mead, "

NEW YORK VOLUNTEERS, COMMISSIONED OFFICERS.

Harry Mead, Assistant Surgeon.

NON-COMMISSIONED OFFICERS.

John F. Mead, Sergeant,   Clifton J. Mead, Corporal.

PRIVATES.

Edward A. Mead,   Frank R. Mead,   John J. Mead,
Edward H. Mead,   Frederick E. Mead,   Orrin W. Mead,
Frank Mead,   George A. Mead,   William Mead.

CHAPTER XIII.

IN MEMORIAM.

THE following is an extract from the funeral sermon for DARIUS MEAD, M.D., delivered at the Second Congregational Church, Greenwich, Connecticut, February 1, 1864, by the Rev. S. B. S. Bissell, of Norwalk, Connecticut:

Darius Mead, son of Joshua Mead and Rachel Knapp, of Round Hill, Greenwich, Connecticut, was born in Greenwich, July 9, 1787. He was fitted for college under the tuition of the venerated Isaac Lewis, D.D., whom he ever greatly revered and loved, and to whom he was much indebted for the formation of his character. He entered Yale College in the year 1803, and was graduated in 1807, at the age of twenty years. Among his classmates were, Thaddeus Betts, lieutenant-governor of Connecticut, and senator in Congress; Aristarchus Champion; John P. Cushman, M.C.; William Dubose, lieutenant-governor of South Carolina; Thomas S. Grimke, LL.D.; William Jay, LL.D.; Alexander Hodgdon Stevens, M.D., LL.D., professor of surgery, and president New York Medical College, and president Medical College, United States; Jacob Sutherland, LL.D., judge Supreme Court, New York; Nathaniel W. Taylor, S.T.D., etc. He studied medicine in Philadelphia, under Dr. Rush, and received his diploma in 1809, in which year he was married to Lydia K., daughter of Elisha Belcher, M.D., of Round Hill. She died sixteen years before him, January 15, 1848. He practised

DR. DARIUS MEAD.

medicine for a few months in New York, but removed to Greenwich in 1810, settling first in the Old Society, but soon removing hither. He united with this church in 1819, soon after the dismission of Rev. Dr. Lewis, under the pastorate of his son of the same name. In the years 1845 and 1846 he represented the Twelfth District in the Senate of Connecticut, being nominated without his seeking or knowledge of the intention. Such are some of the principal facts and events in his personal history.

In his private life, Dr. Mead was a diligent reader of the Bible, making it more and more his companion in his later years. His piety was a deeply settled principle, manifesting itself in an humble, godly, consistent life rather than in many words. Of strong intellect, he had a clear and comprehensive judgment. His mind seemed at once to grasp a subject, however intricate. He turned away with disdain from the frivolous and factitious in life, and was eminently practical and methodical. At the same time, he had a quick and accurate taste, giving him a keen perception of the true and beautiful. While he practised frugality and economy, he despised anything mean and penurious. Although to a casual observer he might, at times, have appeared auster and reserved, he had a very genial and sensitive nature. There was a deep fountain of feeling in his heart, from which gushed out strong and abiding sympathies, pure and ardent affections.

In his home, where he most loved to be, and where he needed to be known in order to be appreciated, Dr. Mead was systematic and energetic in discipline, strict in the training of his children, requiring them sacredly to observe the Sabbath and to commit the Shorter Catechism. Yet he was most affectionate, sympathizing, and self-sacrificing for his children, manifesting a deep interest in their spiritual welfare, constant in family worship, making his home a centre of attraction to them, hallowed in their affections; and to-day they rise up and call him blessed: for what they all are, prosperous, respected in society and in the church of Christ, they are very much indebted, under God, to his exertions and sacrifices, his discipline and example.

In his social and public life, Dr. Mead was a man of stern integrity and unbending uprightness, despising anything like equivocation, insincerity, ostentation, and cunning policy. Of strong will and earnest convictions, he was nevertheless modest and self-denying; finding one of the sources of his greatest happiness in ministering to the happiness of others. He was ever ready to do what he could for the public good, early originating the academy in Greenwich where so many have been educated, and the cemetery where he will sleep with so many of his neighbors. He was always decided on the side of good morals and the general welfare.

As a citizen, Dr. Mead was loyal and patriotic, taking great interest in the efforts of the Government to vindicate the majesty of the Constitution, Laws, and Union against unrighteous rebellion; solicitous for the honor of his country, her delivery from the blighting curse of Slavery, and for the extension and perpetuation of Liberty.

As a Christian, Dr. Mead was punctual in the house of God, often rising very early and riding late on the Sabbath that he might redeem the time of public worship;—jealous for the honor of God and zealous for the peace and prosperity of the Church, the maintenance of her ministry and ordinances, the order and beauty of her house and the building up of the Kingdom of Christ.

As a physician, thoroughly educated and fitted by nature for his profession, he attained a high reputation, and was skilful and successful in an extensive and laborious practice. In no ordinary degree did he sympathize with his patients, bearing their burdens, in cases of danger greatly concerned in regard to them, watching over and studying the changes, features and phases of diseases, and patiently using all the means that the most careful thought and reflection could suggest for their recovery. He was considerate of the poor, giving them his faithful attendance, often visiting them at long distances, through cold storms, dark nights, and wintry blasts, furnishing and preparing their medicines without expectation of reward. He never accumulated wealth in his profession. He was often the minister of spiritual good and consolation to his patients, ever ready to pray with them when it was proper, and to seek the Divine favor upon them.

Born and bred among you, his long and laborious life has been devoted to your service, and he was thoroughly identified with all your interests. Blessed with almost uninterrupted health, and scarcely ever absent from his post, even for a day, continuing active in his profession till the hour he was stricken down by the disease that terminated his life, he was your physician for over half a century.

On the third of December he was suddenly smitten. His disease was acute and painful; but his last anxieties were for the patients he was then visiting, and he could not rest until assured that they should be cared for. After he was attacked he had only the partial use of his faculties; but at intervals he enjoyed religious conversation, and hearing of the Bible and prayer, until he gradually became unconscious, and expired without a groan, January 28, 1864, aged seventy-six years, six months, and nineteen days.

CYRUS P. MEAD, of the John line-Jonathan branch, ¹William, ²John (1), ³Jonathan, ⁴Timothy, ⁵Zebulon, ⁶Martin (1), ⁷Martin (2), ⁸Cyrus P.,-born July 26, 1837, was postmaster at Waterloo, Wisconsin, from the time of his appointment under President Lincoln's first administration, until his death, March 4, 1874. The following obituary notice is taken from the Waterloo paper of that date.

Death, who seldom or never is a welcome visitor, has again called upon us, and in the chilling shadow of his presence, a whole community stands bowed with uncovered heads. This time he has not knocked at the door of the humble and comparatively unknown, whose presence would scarcely have been missed, but with that relentless impartiality which has ever characterized his reign, he has walked into our midst, and laid his mailed hand upon one of our most prominent and respected citizens.

Cyrus P. Mead is no more. He has fallen in the prime of early manhood at the age of thirty-seven years. On the evening of the second, he was engaged in his official duties as postmaster until a late hour. Shortly after retiring for the night he was taken ill. He grew rapidly worse, and at six o'clock P. M. on the fourth his spirit departed to that shoreless future from whence no voyager ever returns.

Mr. Mead had been a resident of this village for thirty years, and for the last fifteen years, was one of our leading business men, during which time he held many public and official positions, all of which he filled with signal ability. We made his acquaintance seventeen years ago. He was ever our friend whom we appreciated among the first of earth; and it is only left for us to pay to his memory a last tribute feeble,— as only words are feeble on such occasions,— but none the less sincere and heartfelt.

Our departed friend was a noble-hearted, generous, consistent, good man. We had frequent opportunities to see him tried, under circumstances where none but the genuine man could have stood the test and come out triumphant; and he was never found wanting in any of the essentials of true manhood. His was a history of kind acts and noble deeds. He planted no thorns nor thistles, to annoy the traveller in life's weary journey, but strewed its rugged path with garlands of unfading flowers. How many will miss his cheerful face, and more than all his active counsel and encouraging words. It may be truthfully said of our departed friend, "It is hard for an enemy to detract from, as for a friend to add to his praise."

The following description of the chapel erected in memory of JULIA C. MEAD of the John line-Benjamin branch, [1] William, [2] John, [3] Benjamin, [4] Benjamin, [5] Thaddeus, [6] Benjamin, [7] Edwin, [8] Julia C.,—is taken from a Brooklyn, New York, paper.

During the whole of yesterday a flag of the Norwegian Merchant Marine floated from a lofty pole planked inside a neat iron railing inclosing the ground on which has just been erected the Bethel of the Norwegian Methodist Episcopal Church, at the southwest corner of President and Van Brunt Streets. The plot of ground is 50 by 100 feet. The Bethel, a neat looking structure, is built with the best quality of brick and finished with blue stone. Its dimensions are 65 feet in length by 38 in width. On either side of the porch at the President Street end of the church are commodious class-rooms, and over them is a large apartment intended to be used for prayer meetings and other similar purposes. The main chapel is nearly 50 feet in length and will seat about 300 persons. It is neatly furnished, well lighted and thoroughly warmed and ventilated. Inserted in the wall at the upper end of the chapel, and on the right hand side of the platform and pulpit is a white marble tablet on which in gilt letters is inscribed:

"In memory of Julia C. Mead, whose devotion to Jesus' poor friends led her father, Edwin Mead, of New York, with his sons, to consecrate this entire property to the Bethel ship, Norwegian Methodist Episcopal Church. To the poor the

Gospel is preached. The abundance of the sea should be converted to Him. Glory be to God alone."

The ground and building cost about $16,000, and as above stated, has been donated by Mr. Edwin Mead, a wealthy shipping merchant of New York, to perpetuate the memory of his deceased daughter, whose death occurred about two years ago. Large numbers of sailors, the majority of whom are Norwegians, are always to be found in that locality, and it was with a view to providing a place for the religious instruction of men of that nationality that the Bethel was built. It takes the place of the floating Bethel that formerly lay at Pier No. 11, North River, New York, and more recently at the foot of Harrison Street, in this city. The society sold it about two years ago, and it now lies at the foot of Fifteenth Street, Jersey City, where it is used as a Bethel by the Protestant Episcopal Church. In one of the class-rooms of the new Bethel is a large supply of Bibles, Testaments and tracts, and pamphlets on religious subjects, printed in the Norwegian language, which are distributed by Mr. Ernst Jackson, an agent of the New York Bible Society, to sailors and others who make application for them.

INDEX.

MEAD FAMILY INDEXED UNDER CHRISTIAN NAMES.

A

Aaron, 76
Aaron B., 97
Abel, 75
Abigail, 10, 19, 24
Abijah, 75
Abner, 76, 84
Abner, Corporal, 76
Abner, Sergeant, 76
Abner B., 99
Abraham, 76, 90
Abraham, 3d, 75
Abraham, Captain, 53, 74
Abraham, Sergeant-Major, 74
Abraham B., 90
Absolom, 99
Addington, John, 84
Adolphus, 99
Alan, 62, 81
Alexandria, O., 34
Allen, 90, 91, 99
Almira, 91
Alston, Anne, 6
Alston, Rowland, 6
Alvin, Corporal, 98
Amasa, 90
Amenia, N. Y., 17, 26
Amos, 30, 76
Amos, Dr., 49, 51, 54-56, 59, 68, 81, 86, 100
Amy, 91
Amzi, 99
Anderson, Major, 96
Andrew, 10, 27, 30, 66, 68
Andrew, Captain, 67
Andrew, Ensign, 74
Andrew, Sergeant, 75
Andrew J., Sergeant, 98
Anna, 60, 61, 63, 64
Annapolis, Md., 100
Anne, of England, 3, 4
Anson, 91
Appleton, O., 34

Applington, Beulah, 29
Appomattox, Va., 112, 113
Arkesden, Eng., 2
Arnold, General Benedict, 77, 85
Aron, 76
Artemus, 90
Arthur J., Lieutenant, 98
Asa C., 99
Asael, 99
Asahel, 35, 36
Asel, 59
Augustus, Quartermaster-Sergeant, 89
Augustus W., Lieutenant, 98
Austin, 99
Austin Friars, Eng., 5
Azor, Sergeant, 74

B

Baker, David, 64
Ballston, N. Y., 26
Barber, J. W., 69
Barnum, Nathaniel, 56
Bates, James, 7
Bates, Johanna, 7
Bates, Richard, 7
Beauregard, General, 106
Beckman, 90
Bedford, N. Y., 21, 85
Belcher, Dr. Elisha, 116
Belcher, Lydia, 116
Bell, Jonathan, 22, 24
Bendish family, Eng., 2
Benjamin, 10, 17, 19, 21, 24, 75, 76, 86, 121
Benjamin, Ensign, 53
Benjamin, Jr., 56
Benjamin, Jr., Lieutenant, 53
Benjamin (1), 54, 121
Benjamin (2), 55, 60, 121
Benjamin (3), 60
Benjamin L., 97
Bennington County, Vt., 34
Bennington, Vt., 33, 77

Index.

Bergen Heights, N. J., 59
Bermuda Hundred, Va., 106, 112
Betsey, 35
Betts, Hon. Thaddeus, 116
Bille, 76
Birney, General, 109
Bissell, Rev. S. B. S., 116
Blackman, Mr., 80
Bond. Ensign Lewis, 39
Boston, Mass., 59, 77
Bowers, John. 20
Bradley, Colonel Philip B., 59
Brograve, Bridget, 2
Brograve, John, 2
Brooklyn, N. Y., 79, 121
Brown, Mary, 10
Brown, Samuel, 4
Broxted, Eng., 3
Bruce, Robert, 80
Brush, Benjamin, 79
Brush, Mary, 79
Buckinghamshire, Eng., 5
Buffalo, N. Y., 39
Bull, Captain, 39
Bunker Hill, Mass., 76
Burnside, General, 101
Bush, 30, 87, 89
Bush, David, 73, 80, 81
Bush, Justus, 56
Bush, Ruth, 56
Bush, William, 56
Bush, Dr. William, 82
Butler, General B. F., 105
Button, Mrs. Philander, 73
Buxton, Clement, 22

C

Caleb, 28, 30
Caleb, Captain, 74
Caleb, Lieutenant, 48, 51, 53
Caleb, Sergeant, 74
Calvin, 75, 76
Cambridgeshire, Eng., 4
Camp, Adjutant, 104
Canada, P. Q., 46, 48
Canton, N. Y., 34
Cary, 33
Cemetery Hill, Va., 111
Centre Rutland, Vt., 32
C. Eugene, Corporal, 98
Chamberlain, Richard, 2
Champion, Aristarchus, 116
Chapel, Eng., 3
Chapin's Farm, Va., 109
Charles, 75, 92, 99
Charles, of England, 2
Charles B., Corporal, 98
Charles D., Colonel, 98
Charles E., Corporal, 98

Charles I., 5
Charles L., 97
Charles, Sergeant, 98
Charles W., Major, 115
Charleston, S. C., 102, 104, 112
Charnell, of England, 4
Charity, 30
Chenango County, N. Y., 26, 29, 30, 91
Chester, N. Y., 30
Chicago, Ills., 92
Clamp, Joan, 2
Clark, 27
Clark, Hannah, 27
Clark, Thomas C., 27
Clifton J., Corporal, 115
Clinton, 91
Close, Elnathan, 67
Close, Samuel, 56
Close, Thomas, 56
Coe, Robert, 9
Coles Island, S. C., 104
Colin, Ellen, 3
Colin, Nicholas, 3
Conneaut Lake, Pa., 38, 39
Cornelius, Hon., 51
Cornwallis, Lord, 77
Cos Cob, Conn., 21, 55, 73
Crab, Richard, 14
Crawford County, Pa., 26, 36, 37, 40, 42, 90
Crishall, Eng., 2, 3
Cristhall Grange, Eng., 3
Croft, Ann, 4
Croft, William, 4
Crown Point, N. Y., 47-50, 59, 84
Crutched Friars, Eng., 5
Curtis, Ruth, 35
Cushman, Hon. John P., 116
Cussewago Creek, Pa., 36, 38, 39
Cussewago Island, Pa., 37
Cyrus, 99
Cyrus H., 98
Cyrus P., 119

D

Dagworths, Eng., 2
Damarius, 84
Danbury, Conn., 56, 77, 83, 85
Daniel, 10, 12, 17, 31, 41, 51, 76, 99
Daniel A., 90
Daniel, Fifer, 75
Daniel, Jr., 99
Daniel M., Major, 97, 99
Darby Road, Va., 110
Darbytown Road, Va., 113
Darius, 35-37, 39, 90
Darius, Dr., 116
Darwin, Wagoner, 98

Index.

Davenport, Major John, 83
David, 7, 10, 19, 21, 24, 56, 75, 76
David, Drummer, 75
David, General, 35, 37, 39, 41, 43, 90
David P., 90
David W., Lieutenant, 97
Davis, Captain P. A., 108
Deep Bottom, Va., 107, 112
Deep Gully, Va., 108, 112
Deep Run, Va., 112
De Mille, Rev. J. H. Hobart, 80
Denton, Humphrey, 68
Denver, Colo., 51
de Prato, Henry, 1
de Prato, Matilda, 1
de Prato, Peter, 1
de Prato, Reginald, 1
de Prato, Richard, 1
de Prato, Robert, 1
de Prato, Roger, 1
de Prato, Stephen, 1
de Prato, Walter, 1
de Prato, William, 1
Derby, Conn., 100
Detroit, Mich., 38, 43
Dinwiddie, Va., 111
Dobbins, Captain Daniel, 43
Dorcas, 84
Dorothy, of England, 4
Drake, Colonel Albert W., 101
Drewry's Bluff, Va., 105, 112
Dryas, H., 99
Dubose, Hon. William, 116
Dumpling Pond, Conn., 15
Duncan, 76
Dupry, Hugh, 42
Dutchess County, N. Y., 17, 26, 30, 32, 50, 51, 90, 91
Dutton Hill, Eng., 3
Dwight, 99

E

Eben, 90
Ebenezer, 10, 17-21, 23-26, 30, 75, 76
Ebenezer, Colonel, 72, 74
Ebenezer, General, 28, 53, 74, 91
Ebenezer, Lieutenant, 53
Ebenezer, Jr., Major, 28, 88, 89
Ebenezer (1), 17, 54
Ebenezer (2), 27, 53, 54
Ebenezer (3), 28, 54
Ebenezer (4), 28, 53, 74, 91
Ebenezer (5), 91
Eber, 90
Edisto Inlet, S. C., 102
Edmund, 76
Edmund, Corporal, 75
Edmund, Sergeant, 89
Edmund W., 90

Edward, 76, 90, 97
Edward, of England, 3
Edward A., 97, 115
Edward C., 99
Edward H., 115
Edward N., 97
Edwin, 121
Edwin F., 99
Eells, Anna, 81
Eells, John, 63
Egbert H., Sergeant, 98
Eli, 36, 76
Elias, 75, 99
Elias A., Lieutenant, 98
Elias S., 29
Elijah, 75
Eliphalet, 49, 55, 91, 97
Elisha, 10, 12, 18, 89
Eliza, 91
Elizabeth, 17, 20
Elizabeth, of England, 3, 4
Elizabeth Neck, Conn., 14, 16, 22
Elkanah, 75
Ella J., 29
Elmdon, Eng., 2, 3
Elmdonbury Hall, Eng., 2
Elnathan, Corporal, 98
Elrington, Edward, 3
Elrington, Humphrey, 3
Ely, 75
Eneck, 75
Enoch, 28, 75
Enoch, Adjutant, 75
Enos, 90
Enos, Major, 89
Epenetus, 75
Erie, Pa., 38, 43, 44, 45
Esben, 75
Essex County, Eng., 1, 2
Esther, of England, 4
Ethan, 76
Experience, 7
Ezbun, Corporal, 89
Ezekiel, 90
Ezekiel, Corporal, 75
Ezekiel, Sergeant, 89
Ezra, 32, 33, 76
Ezra, Ensign, 89
Ezra L., 98

F

Fairfield, Conn., 12, 23, 56
Feaks, Elizabeth, 8
Feaks, Robert, 8, 9
Ferris, James, 22, 55
Ferris, James, Jr., 55
Ferris, Jeffere, 14
Ferry, General O. S., 102
Ferry Point, N. Y., 67

Index.

Field Point, Conn., 87
Finchingfield, Eng., 3
Finney, Janet, 40, 41
Finney, Robert, 40
Fiske, Jonathan, 55
Fitch, William, 3
Fletcher, Corporal, 98
Florence, Italy, 5
Floyer, Matthew, 4
Floyer, Susannah, 4
Flushing, L. I., 63
Flying Cloud, 37
Folly Island, S. C., 104
Fort Bradley, Va., 111
Fort Dearborn, Ills., 92
Fort Edward, N. Y., 48, 52
Fort Franklin, Pa., 37-39
Fort Gregg, Va., 111, 113
Fort Harrison, Va., 109, 113
Fort Lee, N. J., 59
Fort Sumter, S. C., 96
Fort Ticonderoga, N. Y., 47
Fort Wagner, S. C., 104
Fort Washington, N. Y., 59, 77
Foster, General J. G., 100, 102
Francis D., 97
Frank, 115
Frank, Corporal, 98
Frank C., 99
Frank R., 115
Franklin, N. Y., 64
Franklin, 94, 98
Franklin S., 98
Frederick, 97
Frederick A., 99
Frederick E., 115
French Creek, Pa., 36, 39-41
French, General, 101
Frost, Abraham, 12
Fuzzell's Mills, Va., 108, 112

G

Gabriel, 7
Gabriel S., Major, 79
Gardner C., 98
George, 90, 98, 99
George, King, 78
George, of England, 2-4
George II., 6
George A., 98, 115.
George A., Sergeant, 97
George C., Sergeant, 98
George D., Musician, 98
George E., 98
George H., 99
George U., Lieutenant, 98
George W., Regimental Quartermaster, 98
George W., 99, 115.
Gerhardt's Plantation, Va., 110

Germantown, Pa., 85
Gershom, 48-51
Gibbons, General, 111
Gideon, 56, 59, 99
Gilbert, 76
Gill, William, 40
Gillchrist, Captain William, 51
Gillmore, General, 105
Glascock, Jane, 3
Glascock, John, 3
Gloucester Point, Va., 104
Goldsboro, N. C., 101, 102, 112
Goodman, 7
Goodyear, Colonel E. D. S., 111
Gould, Mr., 12
Grant, General U. S., 111
Granville, O., 33, 34
Great Easton, Eng., 3
Greeley, Colonel E. S., 104, 106, 110
Green Bay, Wis., 92
Green, General, 59
Green, James, 47
Gregg, 38
Greenwich, Conn., 7, 10, 12, 16, 17, 19, 20, 23, 25-32, 46-53, 55, 56, 58, 59, 67-69, 78, 80, 85, 87, 90, 99, 116
Greenwich Point, Conn., 8, 25, 87, 88
Grigg, Captain John, 82
Grimke, Thomas S., LL.D., 116
Guernsey, Sarah, 30

H

Haight, Miriam, 91
Half Town, 37
Halsey, Corporal, 75
Hamilton, N. C., 101
Hanford, 97
Hanford, Levi, 63
Hanford, Mary, 81
Hanford, Captain Samuel, 48, 84
Hanford, William B., 64
Hannah, 10, 19, 24, 84, 91
Hardey, Richard, 12, 16
Hardey, Ruth, 16
Hardy, Commodore, 87, 91
Harlem Heights, N. Y., 77, 79
Harmer, General, 39
Harrison, General, 44
Harry, Assistant-Surgeon, 115
Harry A., Musician, 115
Hart, Colonel Jonathan, 48, 51, 52
Hartford, Conn., 47, 100, 112
Harvey, 90
Haslingfield, Eng., 4
Hatcher's Run, Va., 111, 113
Havana, Cuba, 50, 114
Helon, 89
Hempstead, L. I., 11, 12, 14
Henary, 75
Henham, Eng., 3

Index. 127

Henry, 19, 34, 47, 76, 89, 99
Henry, Corporal, 89
Henry, Jr., 75, 90
Henry VI., 2
Henry, of England, 3, 4
Henry II., 97, 99
Henry T., Adjutant, 98
Henry W., 99
Hertford, Eng., 1
Hertfordshire, Eng., 2
Heusted, Angell, 9, 14
Heusted, Angell, Jr., 20, 22
Heusted, Robert A., 9
Hewitt, Elizabeth, 4
Hewitt, William, 4
Hezekiah, Captain, 75
Hibbard, 97
Hickerson, Captain Francis G., 111
Hill, Captain Ebenezer, 59
Hiram, Ensign, 89
Hitchcock, Captain Amos, 50
Hobby, Elizabeth, 81
Hobby, Captain Thomas, 47-50, 91
Holland, 5
Holley, Edward P., 73
Holmes, Captain James, 50
Holmes, Mercy, 84
Horseneck, Conn., *see* Greenwich
Hosea, 26
How, Peter, 82
Howe, Captain Isaac, 99
Hubbell, Captain Samuel, 49
Hubbell, Lieutenant, 85
Hudson, N. Y., 35, 90
Hunter, Colonel, 43
Huntingdon, Eng., 2
Huntington, L. I., 63
Huntington, N. I., 59
Husted, William A., 73
Hyde, Dr. Fred, 60

I

Isaac, 75, 76, 90
Isaac, Jr., 90
Isaac, Captain Isaac, 49
Isaac L., 72, 74, 97
Isaac N., Corporal, 98
Isaiah, 26
Isaiah, Sergeant, 75
Ismael, 76
Israel, 7, 26, 29, 75, 76, 91
Israel, Corporal, 89
Israel, Jr., 76

J

Jabez, 54, 56, 74, 89, 91
Jabez, Jr., 55
Jackson, Ernest, 122
Jacob, 34, 75, 99
Jacob, Corporal, 76, 89
Jacob, Ensign, 75
Jacob, Fifer, 76
James, 30, 33, 48, 55, 56, 75, 76, 84, 89, 90, 99
James, Colonel, 32, 33, 76, 84
James, Ensign, 46, 48
James, Lieutenant, 49
James, of England, 4
James A., 99
James E., 98
James H., 90
James M., 99
James McF., 99
James P., 99
James S., 99
J. S., 99
James Island, S. C., 103
James River, Va., 105
Jane, of England, 3
Jared, 68, 75
Jasper, 30
Jasper, Lieutenant, 74
Jasper, Regimental Quartermaster, 74
Jay, William, LL.D., 116
Jeffers, Captain, 41
Jehiel, Ensign, 75
Jehiel, Lieutenant, 74
Jemima, 28, 56
Jeremiah, 30, 56, 75, 76, 84, 90, 99
Jeremiah, Jr., Ensign, 74
Jeremiah C., 99
Jeremiah O., 98
Jersey City, N. J., 59
Jespor, 75
Jesse, 49, 50
Jesse, Ensign, 74
Jesse H., Sergeant, 89
Jeudethan, 90
Joan, of England, 3
Job, 89
Job, Captain, 75
Job, Jr., 76
Job (1), 26
Job (2), 26
Joel, 76, 89
Joel, Captain, 75
Johanna, 7
John, 10-12, 14, 16, 17, 20, 29, 35-37, 50, 53, 54, 56, 75, 76, 90, 91, 99, 121
John, Blacksmith, 98
John, Colonel, 28
John, Drum-Major, 62, 75
John, King, 1
John, Lieutenant, 98
John, of England, 2-4
John (1), 10-12, 14-17, 19, 20, 23, 25, 26, 30-32, 35, 54, 84, 119, 121
John (2), 10, 12, 16, 17, 19, 20, 23, 26, 30, 54

Index.

John (3), Captain, 17, 20, 22, 30, 53, 54
John (4), General, 53-55, 61, 74, 77, 78, 86, 91
John (5), 62
John, 3d, 62, 75, 80, 81
John A., 98
John B., Colonel, 98
John B. T., Adjutant, 98
John D., 98
John D., Musician, 97
John F., 99
John F., Sergeant, 115
John J., 115
John M., Corporal, 97
John P., 90
Johnson Place, Va., 110
Johnson Plantation, Va., 113
John's Island, S. C., 103
Jonah, 75
Jonah, Sergeant, 75
Jonas, 56
Jonathan, 10, 17-21, 23, 26, 32, 35, 75, 76, 84, 90, 119
Jonathan (1), 26, 29, 32, 35
Jonathan (2), 26, 29, 35
Jonathan (3), 29
Jonathan (4), 30
Jones' Landing, Va., 107
Joseph, 10-12, 16-20, 23, 24, 29, 35, 36, 49, 54, 75, 76, 91, 99
Joseph (1), 17, 29, 84, 91
Joseph (2), 17, 26, 29, 91
Joseph, Corporal, 48
Joseph, Drummer, 75
Joseph, Ensign, 48, 49
Joseph E., 90, 91
Joseph N., Lieutenant, 98
Joseph W., 99
Joshua, 26, 48, 50, 99, 116
Joshua, Sergeant, 75
Josiah, 50, 55, 56, 75, 76
Josiah, Sergeant, 89
Jotham, 90
Jothem, 75
Judson, Corporal, 98
Julia, 91
Julia C., 121

K

Katharine, of England, 2
Keeler, Captain Samuel, 59
Kent County, Eng., 7
King, 76
King, Mercy, 26
Kinston, N. C., 101, 112
Knapp, Rachel, 116
Knapp, Timothy, 65

L

Lafayette, 99
Lafayette, General Marquis, 69
Lake George, N. Y., 47
Lake Waccabuc, N. Y., 28, 30
Laurel Hill Church, Va., 113
Law, Jonathan, 52
Law, Richard, 11
Lawrence, 99
Leander, Sergeant, 89
Lee, General, 97
Leggett, Colonel Robert, 101, 104
Leicester County, Eng., 4
Lemuel D., 99
Levi, 75, 76, 90
Lewis, 51, 90
Lewis, Beale, 84
Lewis, Commodore, 88
Lewis, Isaac, D.D., 116
Lewis M., 99
Lewisboro, N. Y., 27
Lexington, Mass., 76
Leyden, Netherlands, 5
Libbeus, Corporal, 75
Libbeus, Sergeant, 75
Licking County, O., 34
Lincoln, Hon. Abraham, 96
Lockwood, 75
Lockwood, Elizabeth, 78
Lockwood, Gershom, 22
London, Eng., 2, 3
Long Island, N. Y., 77, 79
Louis, 76
Louisa S., 99
Lucius H., 99
Luke, 89
Lydd, Eng., 7
Lydia, 7
Lyman, 99

M

McClellan, General, 97
McFarland, James E., 37
McHenry County, Ills., 92
McNeil, Captain Archibald, 48, 49
Mackinaw, Mich., 43
Maher, John, 72
Mallett, Colonel, 101
Mamaroneck, N. Y., 68
Manchester, Conn., 102
Manchester, Vt., 34
Margaret, of England, 2, 3
Maria, 41
Marilda, 91
Marlborough Church, Eng., 4
Mark, Rev., 72
Marsel, 76
Marshall, 76

Index.

Marshall, John, 56
Marshall, John, Jr., 56
Marshe, Ruth, 6
Marshel, 76
Martha, 10, 11
Martial, 76
Martin, 27, 89, 90, 99, 119
Mary, 10, 12, 19, 24, 60, 62, 63
Matching, Eng., 3
Mather, Abel, 81
Matthew, 48, 56, 75
Matthew, of England, 2
Matthew, Captain, 53, 54, 74, 80
Matthew, Colonel, 48, 50, 56, 74, 77, 84, 86
Matthew, Ensign, 50
Matthew, Quartermaster, 48
Matthew, Rev., of England, 4
Mead Township, Pa., 39
Mead's Mills, Vt., 32
Mead's Point, Conn., 87
Meadville, Pa., 10, 35, 36, 40, 41
Mehetable, 80, 81
Mercer County, Pa., 37, 39
Mercy, 26, 33, 84
Merritt, Abraham, 81
Merritt, Shubel, 58
Messenger, Andrew, 9
Mianus, Conn., 58
Mianus River, Conn., 15
Michael, Captain, 89
Mifflin, Hon. Thomas, 42
Mills, Amos, 82
Montreal, Canada, 49
Morris D., 98
Morris Island, S. C., 102, 104
Moses, 76
Mott, Adam, 15
Mounteneys, Eng., 2
Mount Vernon, N. Y., 68
Munrow, Amos, 55

N

Nancy, 91
Nansemond County, Va., 10
Naples, Italy, 5
Napoleon, 99
Nathan, 17, 20, 26, 32, 75, 76
Nathaniel, 10, 18, 19, 21, 22, 24, 30, 55, 56, 76, 83, 90, 99
Nathaniel, 3d, 75
Nathaniel, Lieutenant, 75
Nathaniel, Sergeant, 74
Nehemiah, 26, 53, 55, 76
Nehemiah, Lieutenant, 54
Nelson H., 99 ,
Nemiah, Jr., 75
Nemiah, Sergeant, 74
Nesbit, John, 5

Netus, 75
Neuse River, N. C., 101
Nevill, Colonel, 39
Newbern, N. C., 101, 102, 112
New Canaan, Conn., 61, 63
New Haven, Conn., 104
Newmarket Heights, Va., 109, 113
New London, Conn., 77
New Orleans, La., 88
New Purchase, N. Y., 85
New Rochelle, N. Y., 71
New York, N. Y., 63, 66, 68, 77, 79, 110, 122
Nicholas, 94
Nine Partners, N. Y., 26, 30, 32, 90, 91
Noah, 76
Norman, 99
Normandy, France, 1
North Greenwich, Conn., 60, 78, 80
Northumberland County, Pa., 26, 35-37, 90
Nortofts, Eng., 3, 4
Norwalk, Conn., 47-50, 54-56, 84, 116

O

Obadiah, 60
Obadiah, Sergeant, 89
Obediah, 75
Ogden, Captain Jonathan, 50
Old Greenwich, see Sound Beach
Oliver, Fifer, 75
Orison, Captain, 89
Orrin W., 115
Oscar, 99
Oswegatchie, N. Y., 49
Otis, General John L., 100, 102
Otter Creek, Vt., 32, 33
Oxfordshire, Eng., 4

P

Padua, Italy, 5
Palo Alto, Tex., 94
Pardee, Colonel, 101
Paris, France, 115
Paschel, 76
Patience, 7
Patrick, Captain Daniel, 8, 9
Peck, Abraham, 83
Peck, Rev. Jeremiah, 16
Peck, Jonathan, 80, 83
Peck, Jonathan R., 83
Peck, Mehetabel, 80
Perry, Commodore O. H., 43-45
Peter, 54, 55, 66, 86, 90
Peter, Sergeant, 74
Peter C., 99
Petersburg, Va., 11, 108, 113

Index.

Pettibone, Colonel Ira W., 101
Petty, Charnell, 4
Petty, Elizabeth, 4
Phebe, 60
Philadelphia, Pa., 116
Philip, 76, 90
Philip, Corporal, 76
Philip, of England, 4
Pittsburgh, Pa., 40
Pittsford, Vt., 33
Plaisted, General, 105, 110
Platt, 59
Plymouth, N. C., 101
Port Walthal Junction, Va., 105
Potter, Anna, 30
Potter, Hannah, 10, 15
Potter, William, 15, 22
Poughkeepsie, N. Y., 99
Proctor, General, 44
Putnam, General Israel, 18, 69
Put's Hill, Conn., 78
Pytches, William, 3

Q

Quaker Ridge, Conn., 60
Quebec, Canada, 76, 85

R

Rachel, 30, 55
Ralph, 90
Ralph S., 98
Ransom H., 99
Rawle's Mills, N. C., 101
Ray, ——, 38
Rebecca, 26
Redding, Conn., 54, 55, 71
Reginald, of England, 2
Reuben, 19, 75
Reynolds, Gideon, 56
Rheumah, 91
Richard, 10, 12, 27, 31, 68, 69, 75, 76, 84, 100
Richard, Dr., of England, 5, 13
Richard K., 11
Richard K., Colonel, 10
Richardson, John, 11
Richmond, Va., 107
Ridgefield, Conn., 55, 63
Roanoke Island, N. C., 100, 101, 112
Robert, Earl of Sussex, 2
Robert, of England, 2-4
Robert P., 115
Rogers, 89
Rome, Italy, 5
Rouen Castle, Normandy, 2
Rowell, Eng., 3
Royal, 98
Rufus, 76
Rufus, Jr., 98
Rufus, Jr., Sergeant, 89
Rufus N., 98
Russell, Colonel Charles L., 100
Ruth, 17, 30, 35
Rutland, Vt., 32, 33
Rye, N. Y., 58, 71

S

Sag Harbor, L. I., 77
St. Augustine, Fla., 104, 112
St. Clair, General, 39
St. Helena Island, S. C., 102
St. John, Hannah, 84
St. Johns, Canada, 85
St. Lawrence County, N. Y., 30, 34
Salem, N. Y., 27
Sally, 30
Samantha, 84
Samford, Elizabeth, 3
Samford, Robert, 3
Sampson, Judith, 33
Samuel, 10, 18, 19, 22, 24, 30, 55, 89, 90
Samuel, Fifer, 75
Samuel, Lieutenant, 53
Samuel, Jr., 90
Samuel, of England, 5
Sarah, 7, 30, 37, 56, 84, 91
Saratoga, N. Y., 77
Saratoga County, N. Y., 26
Satterfield, Rev. Mr., 37
Sawpits, N. Y., 71
Scoful, Hannah, 24
Seabrook Island, S. C., 103, 112
Seaman, Hon., 51
Seaman M., 115
Selah, 76, 87, 89
Sellick, Captain Jonathan, 55
Sely, Sergeant, 75
Seneca, 99
Seth, 81, 99
Seth, Captain, 89
Seymour, Captain Seth, 63
Shadrach, 30, 90
Shadrach F., Corporal, 89
Shaffer, Colonel J. W., 107, 108
Shenango Creek, Pa., 39
Shippan Point, Conn., 15, 22
Sidney, Captain, 98
Sidney M., 99
Silas, 76
Silas, Jr., 75, 76
Silas E., 98
Simpson, Captain John, 43
Singleton, Thomas, 5
Slocum's Creek, N. C., 101
Smith, 75, 76, 90, 98
Smith, John, 3

Index.

Sniffen, Mary A., 81
Solomon, 28, 75, 90
Solomon, Rev., 27, 28
Solomon S., 60
Somersetshire, Eng., 2
Sound Beach, Conn., 9, 14, 16, 17, 25, 88
South Bainbridge, N. Y., 29
South Norwalk, Conn., 63
South Salem, N. Y., 27, 28
Spicer, Mrs., 63
Spring Hill, Va., 108
Staffordshire, Eng., 4
Stagg, Captain, 7
Stamford, Conn., 8-12, 14, 22, 24, 52, 55, 69, 71, 72
Stanwich, Conn., 27, 82
Stark, ——, 33
States M., 90
Stephen, 32, 33, 50, 54-56, 75, 76, 84, 90, 99
Stephen, Captain, 54
Stephen, Corporal, 75
Stephen, Lieutenant, 54
Stepney, Eng., 5
Stevens, Dr. Alexander H., 116
Stevenson, Colonel T. G., 102
Stillman, Colonel, 85
Strawberry Plains, Va., 108, 112
Strong, Rev. Benjamin, 27
Strong, Hannah, 27
Studwell, Thomas, 14
Sunbury, Pa., 36
Sutherland Falls, Vt., 32, 33
Sutherland, Hon. Jacob, 116
Susannah, 55
Sussex County, Eng., 2
Swartout, Captain Jacobus, 51
Sylvanus, 90
Sylvanus, Captain, 49, 58, 60, 69, 74, 88
Sylvanus, Corporal, 49, 59
Sylvester, 99

T

Tameson, 84
Tarboro, N. C., 101
Taylor, Rev. Nathaniel W., 116
Thadd, 99
Thaddeus, 75, 76, 85, 121
Thaddeus, ae. 76, 75
Thaddeus, Captain, 49, 56
Thaddeus, Commissary, 48
Thaddeus, Lieutenant, 47, 48
Theodosia, 27, 60
Theophilus, 75
Thespt., Fifer, 75
Thomas, 75, 99
Thomas, Jr., 2, 89

Thomas, of England, 2, 3
Thomas A., Colonel, 69, 99
Thomas G., 99
Thomas K., 92
Thomas R., Captain, 97, 100
Thompson, 91
Thompson, Colonel, 30, 89, 90
Throgg's Neck, N. Y., 87, 91
Ticonderoga, N. Y., 48, 49, 51, 59, 84
Timothy, 32-34, 76, 84, 119
Timothy, Jr., 76
Timothy (1), 32, 33, 119
Timothy (2), 32, 34
Timothy 3d, 76
Titus, 30, 56, 65, 75
Townsend, Cole, 81
Treat, Sallomon, 22, 24
Trenton, N. C., 101
Trimble, James, 42
Truman, 76
Truman, Fifer, 76
Trumbull, Chaplain, 104
Tryon, Governor, 19, 70, 77, 85
Turner, Captain, 8, 9
Tyler, 90
Tyler, Corporal, 89

U

Upton, Eng., 3
Uriah, 75
Uriah, Fife-Major, 75
Uriah, Sergeant, 74
Utrecht, Netherlands, 5

V

Valley Forge, Pa., 85
Van Denbergh, Captain Peter, 50
Van Horne, ——, 38
Van Horne, Ensign, 40
Vincent, General, 45
Volney, 99

W

Wakeman, Rev. Mr., 12
Walker, General, 106
Walter, 81
Walter C., 51
Walter F., 99
Walter H., 90
Walthal Junction, Va., 105, 112
Walton, 99
Walton, N. Y., 63, 64, 79
Ward, Andrew, 9
Ward, B., 98
Wardour, Jane, 3
Wardour, William, 3
Warren, 99

Index.

Warren County, N. Y., 30
Warren County, Pa., 37
Washington, D. C., 43, 94, 95
Washington, N. C., 100
Washington, General George, 10, 66, 86
Waterbury, Conn., 27
Waterbury, Captain David, 48
Waterbury, Jno., 11
Waterloo, Wis., 119
Watson, N., 98
Wayne General, 39, 40
Wendon Lofts, Eng., 2
Wendy, Dorothy, 4
Wendy, Thomas, 4
Westchester County, N. Y., 27, 28, 30, 50, 51
West Creek, Vt., 33
West Point, N. Y., 85
West Rutland, Vt., 32, 33
Wethersfield, Conn., 8, 9
Whaley, John, 3
Whelpley, Betty, 56
Whelpley, Phebe, 84
White, Captain Stephen, 39, 48, 51, 52
Whitehall, N. C., 102, 112
White Plains, N. Y., 77, 79
Whiting, Frederic, 83
Whitman, 59, 88
Whitman S., Hon., 17
Wier Bottom, Va., 106
William, 7, 8, 10, 11, 14, 29, 33, 42, 75, 76, 84, 89-91, 99, 115, 119, 121
William, of England, 3, 4
William, Corporal, 89
William, Rt. Rev., 11
William, Surgeon, 75
William A., 99
William B., Sergeant, 89, 98
William C., 90
William H., 99, 115
William R., 90

William W., Captain, 98
Williams, Richard, 9
Williams, Robert, 15
Williams, Sophia F., 29
Williamstown, N. C., 101
Wilmot, Edward, 6
Wilson, Agnes, 35
Wilson, Edward, 4
Wilson, Elizabeth, 4
Wilson, Janet, 35
Wilson, John, 35
Wilton, Conn., 54, 84
Windsor, Conn., 8, 101
Winsted, Conn., 101
Wolcott, A., 98
Wood, Jonah, 59
Wood, Sybil, 59
Wooster, Colonel David, 47-49
Wooster, Captain Joseph, 46
Wyllys, George, 52
Wyoming County, Pa., 26, 35, 36

Y

Yorktown, Va., 77

Z

Zaccheus, 75
Zachariah, 10, 12, 17, 22, 24, 26, 76
Zachariah, Sergeant, 97
Zadee, 90
Zadoc, 90
Zadock, 90
Zalmuna, 90
Zalock, 76
Zebibediah, 76
Zebulon, 32, 33, 76, 119
Zebulon, Jr., 76
Zebulon, Lieutenant, 50
Zelek, 76

ImTheStory.com

Personalized Classic Books in many genre's

Unique gift for kids, partners, friends, colleagues

Customize:
- Character Names
- Upload your own front/back cover images (optional)
- Inscribe a personal message/dedication on the inside page (optional)

Customize many titles Including
- Alice in Wonderland
- Romeo and Juliet
- The Wizard of Oz
- A Christmas Carol
- Dracula
- Dr. Jekyll & Mr. Hyde
- And more...